Color Fun Patterns

Coloring Book

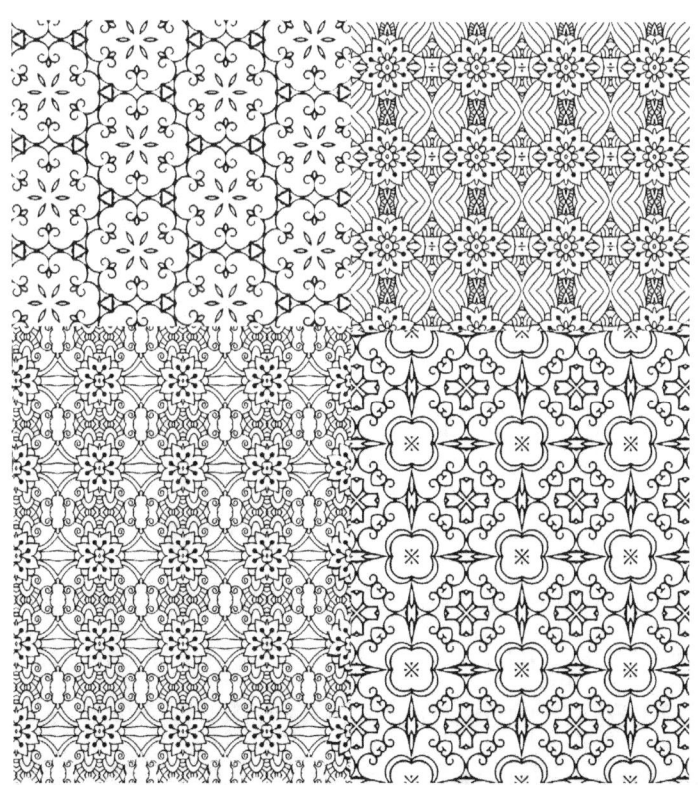

MacGabini Fun Books

For best quality of your artwork, we recommend you place a blank paper or card between the page you are coloring and the next

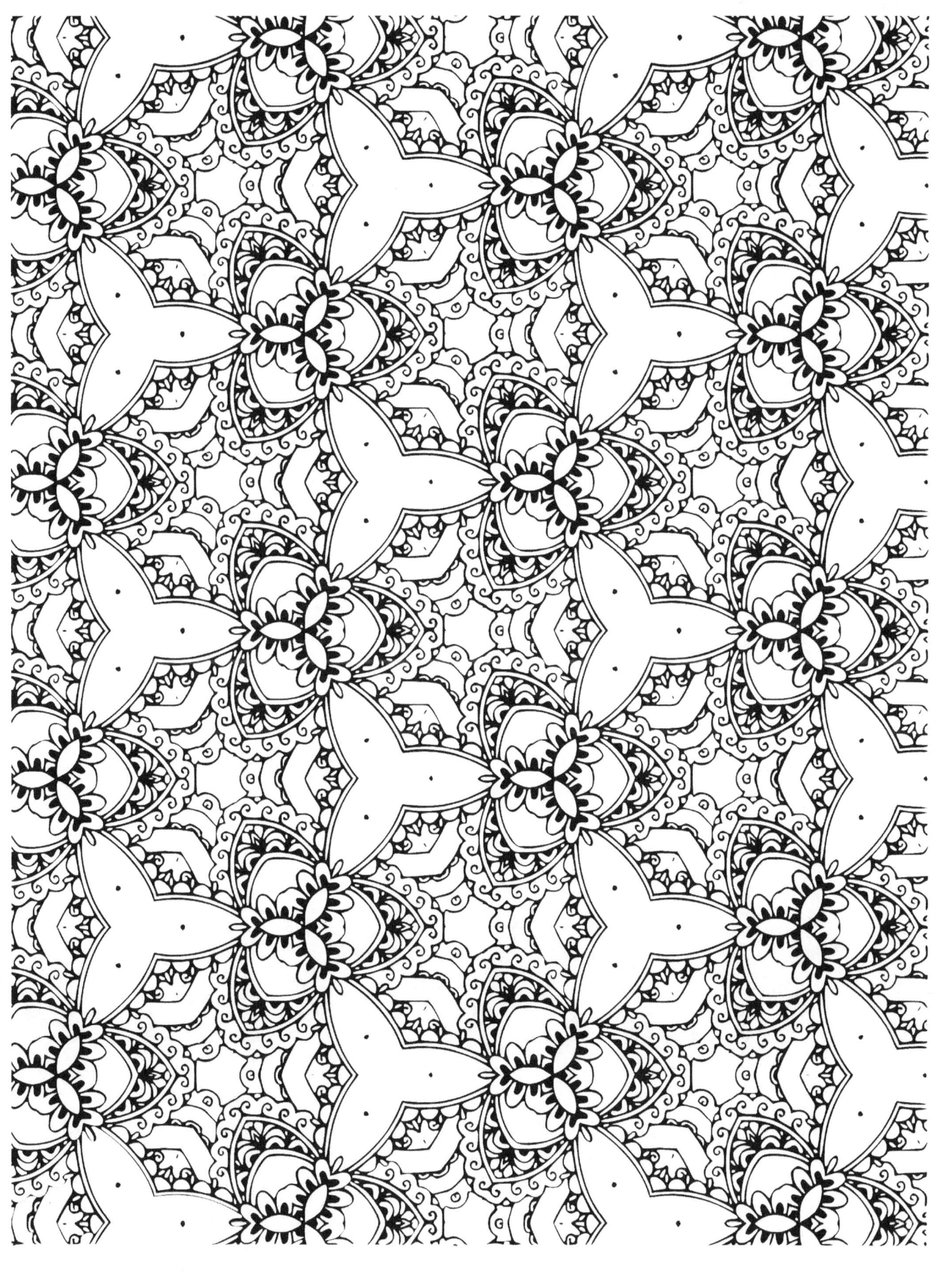

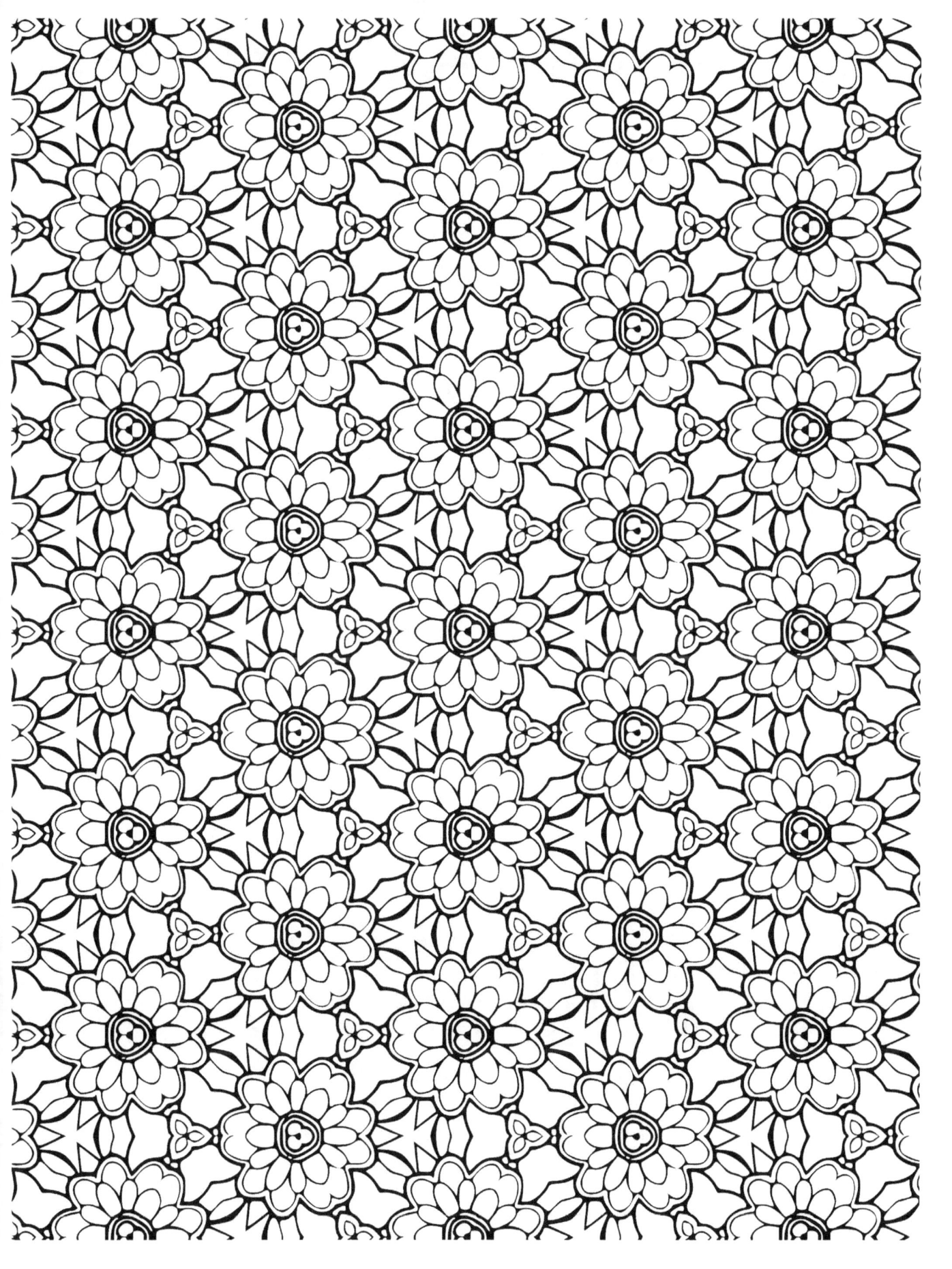

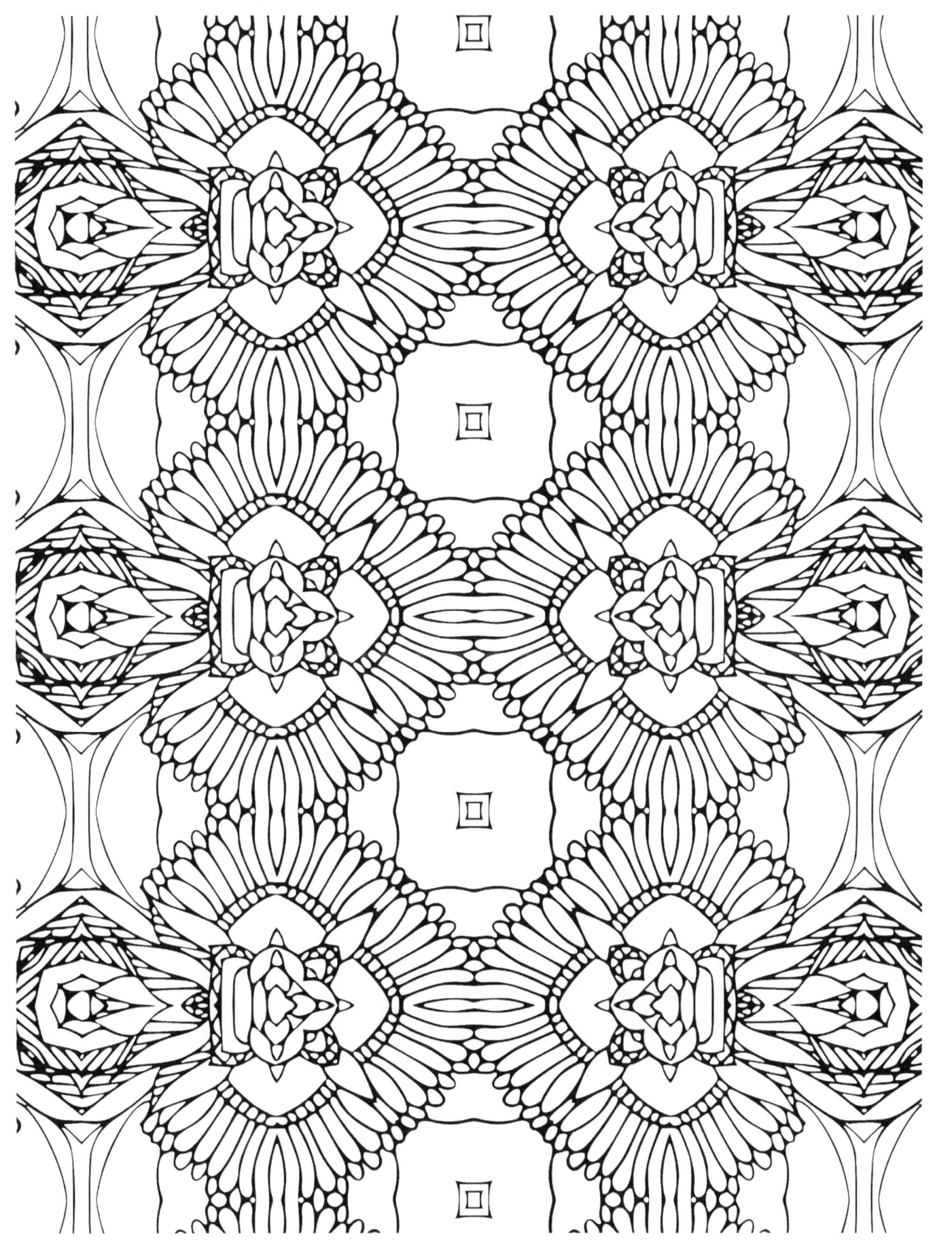

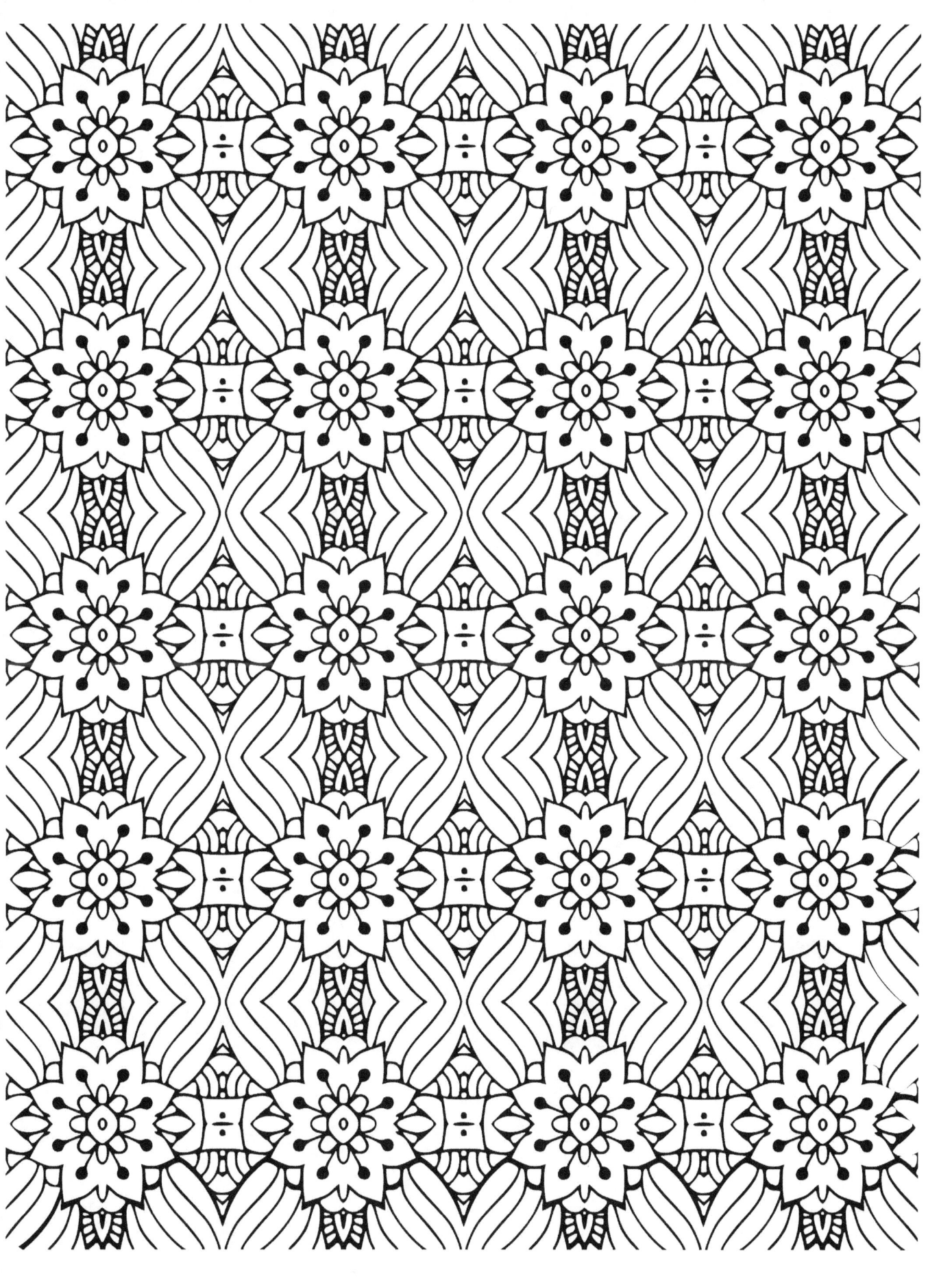

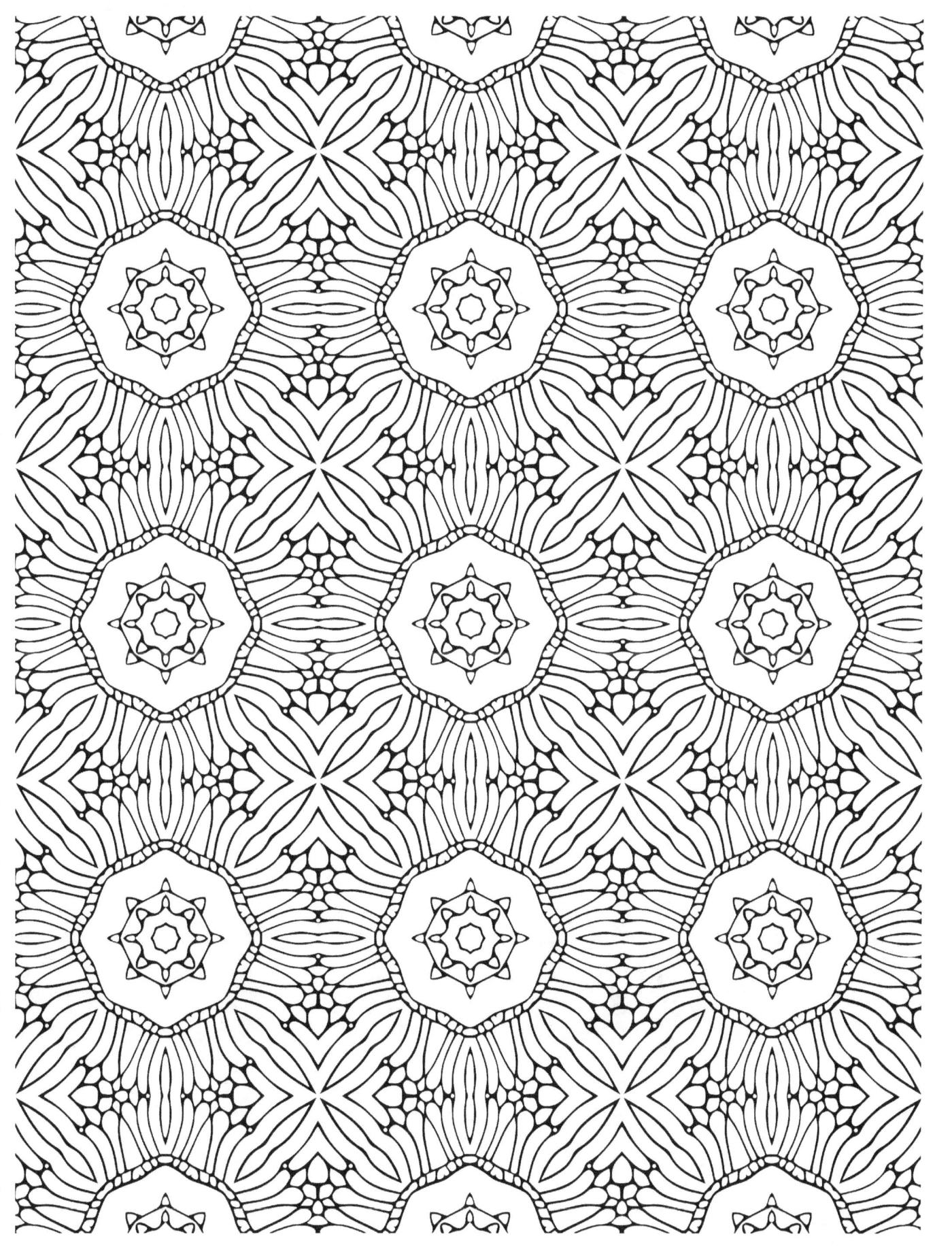

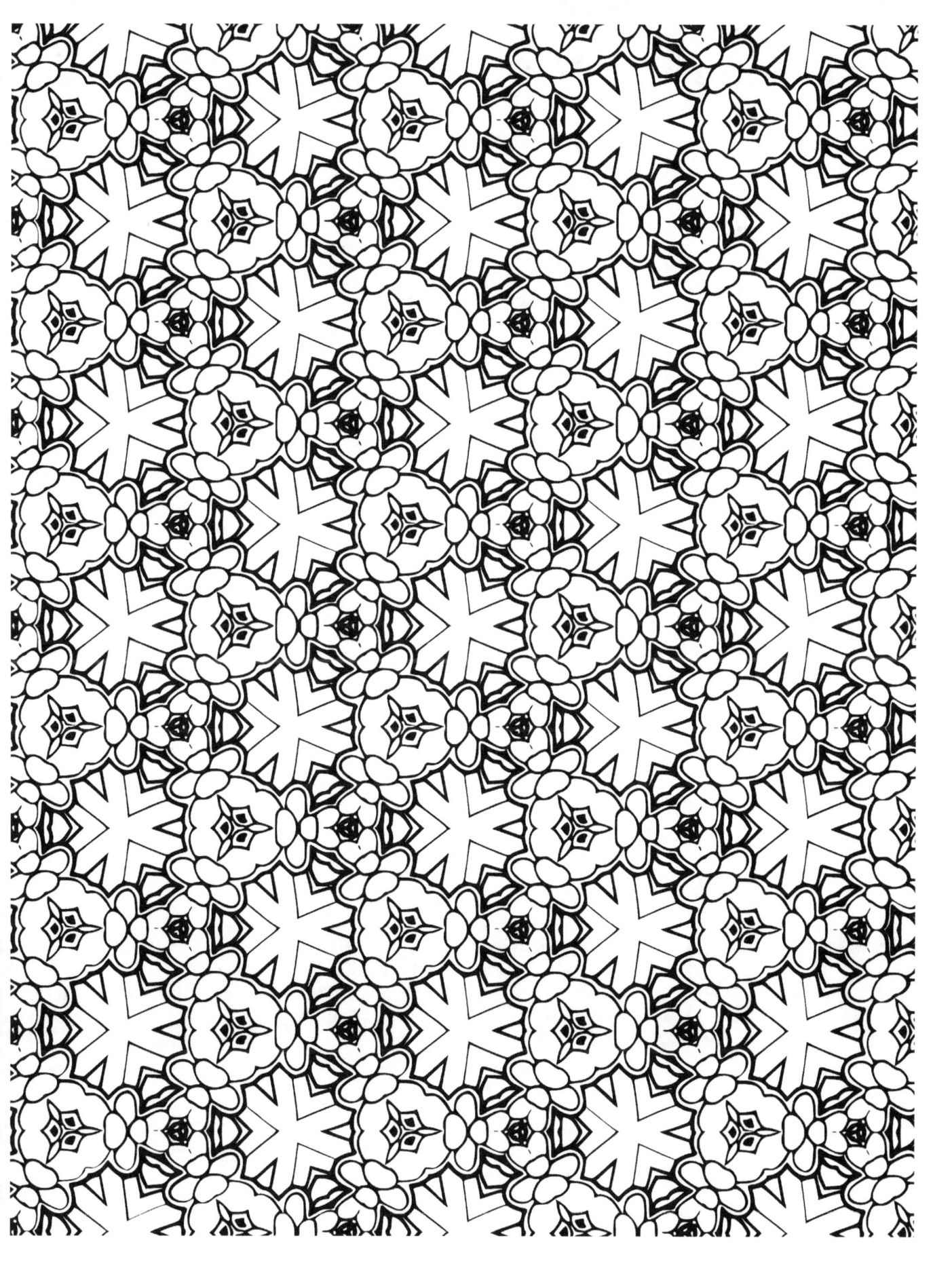

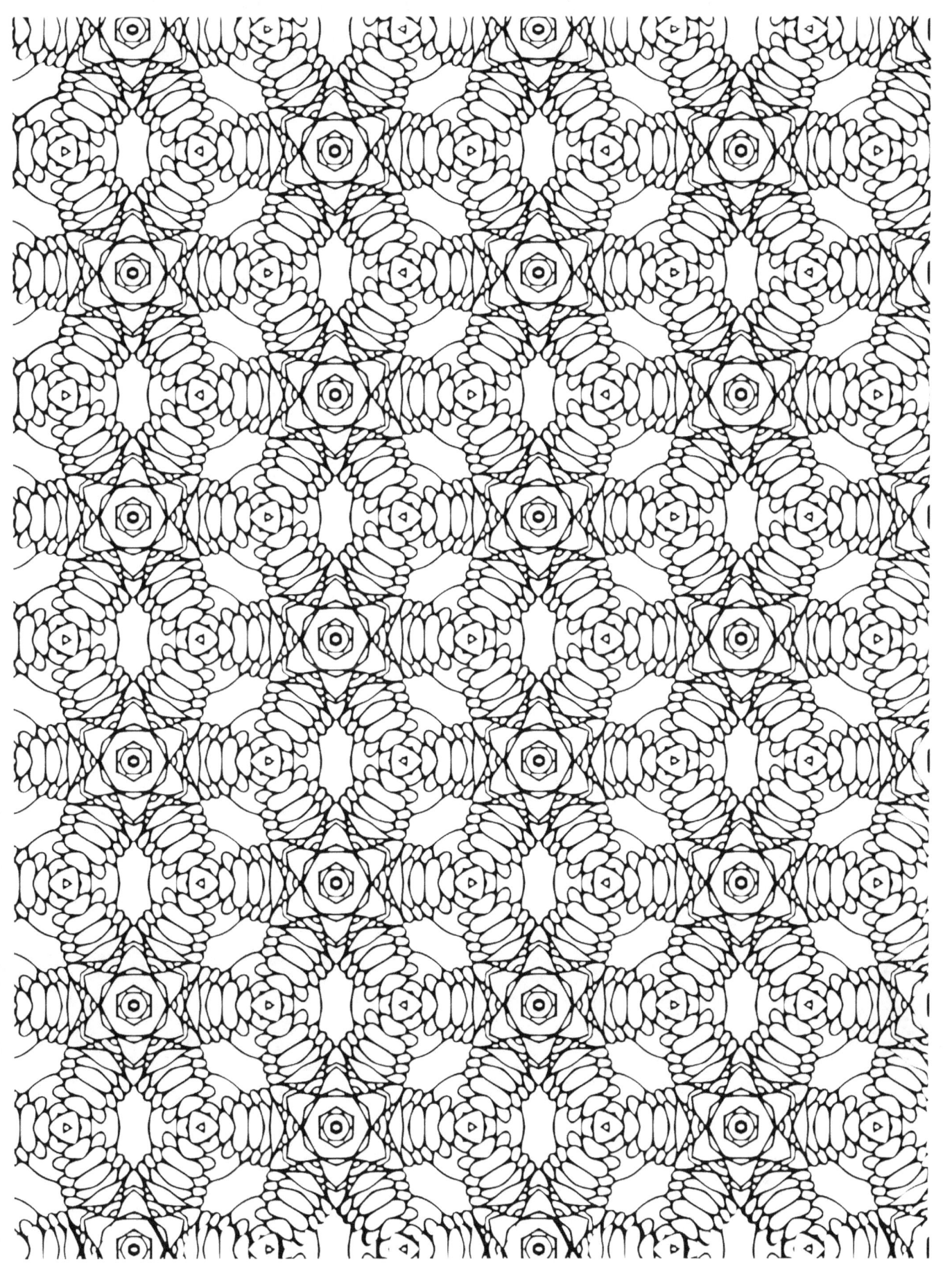

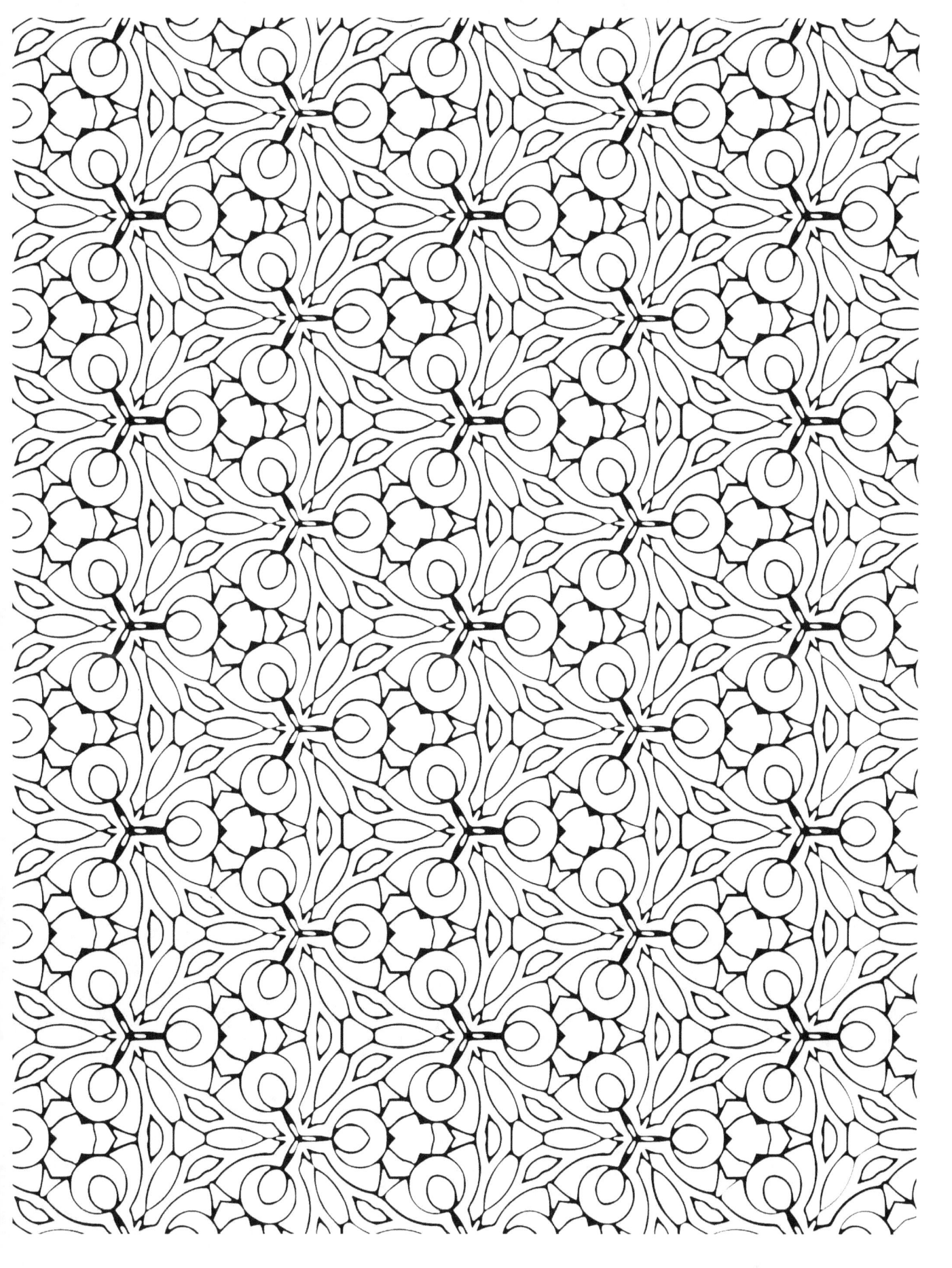

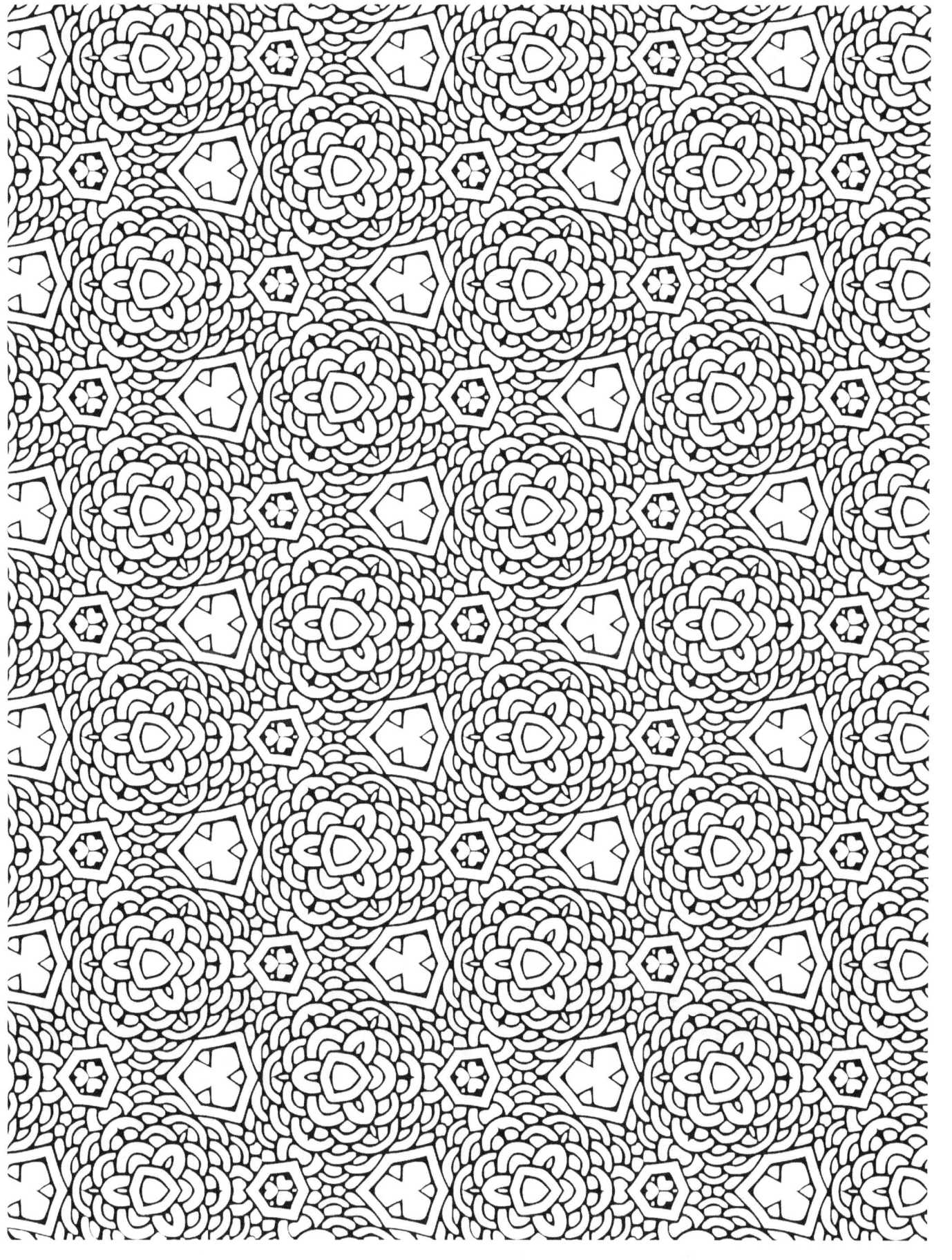

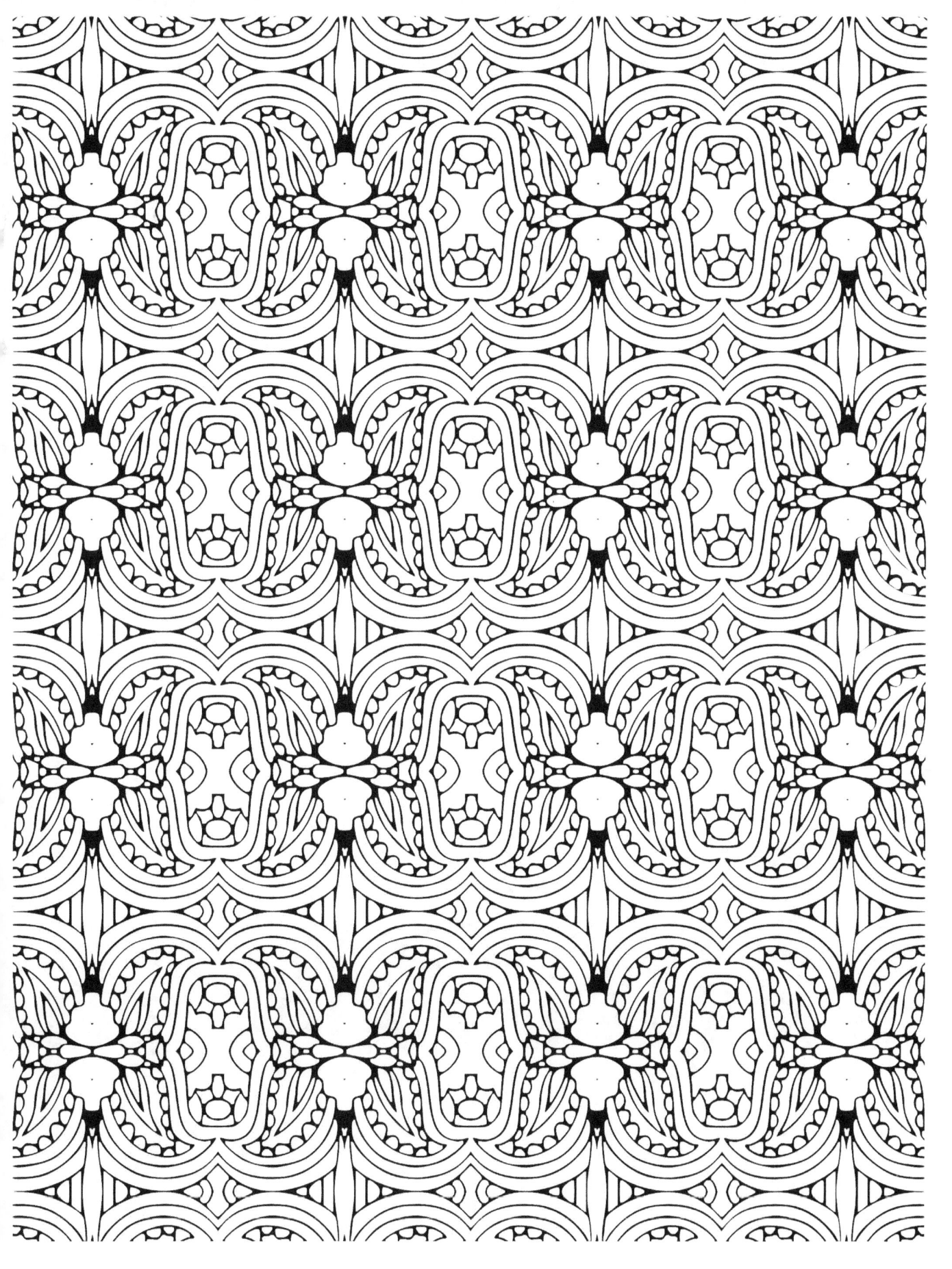

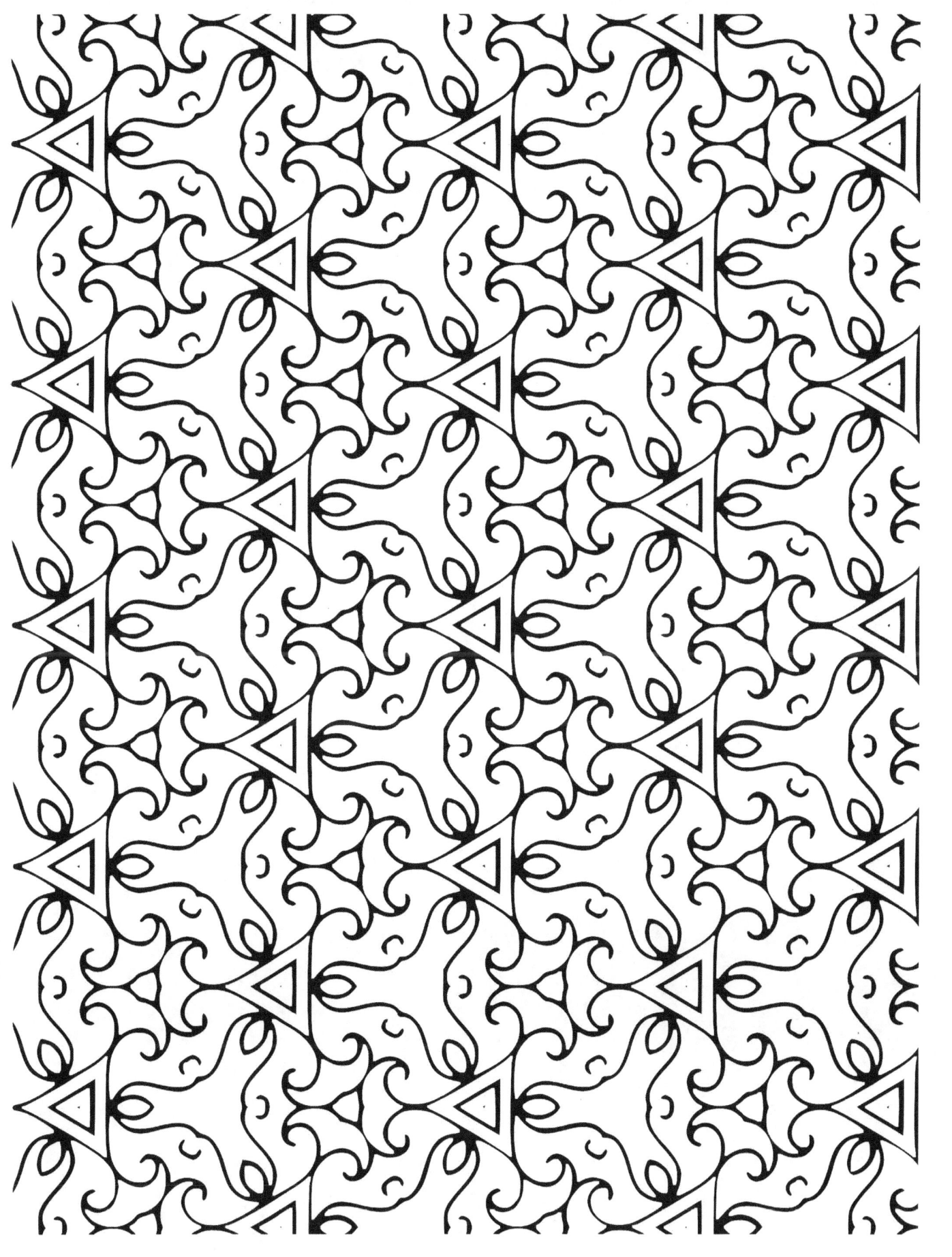

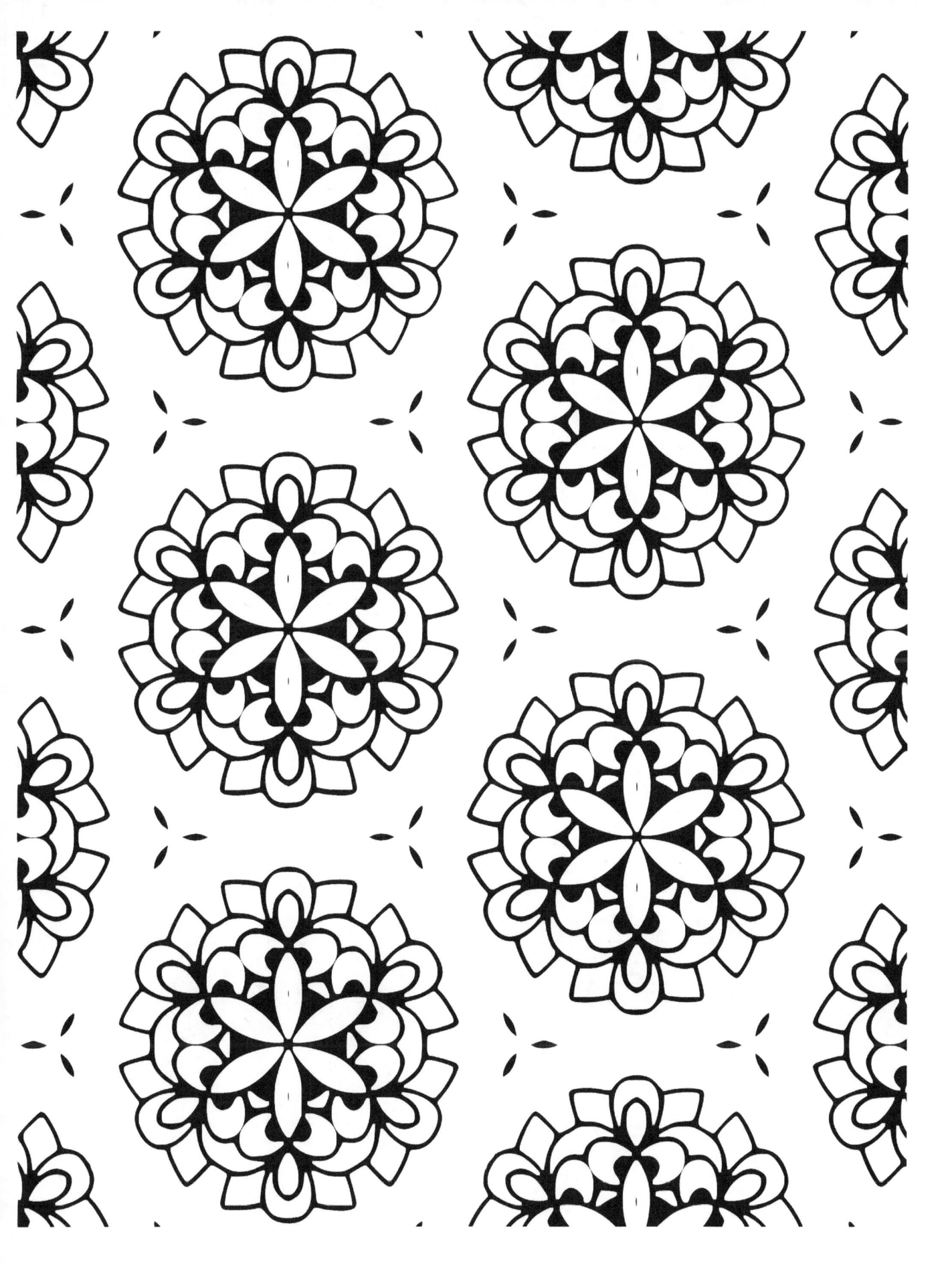

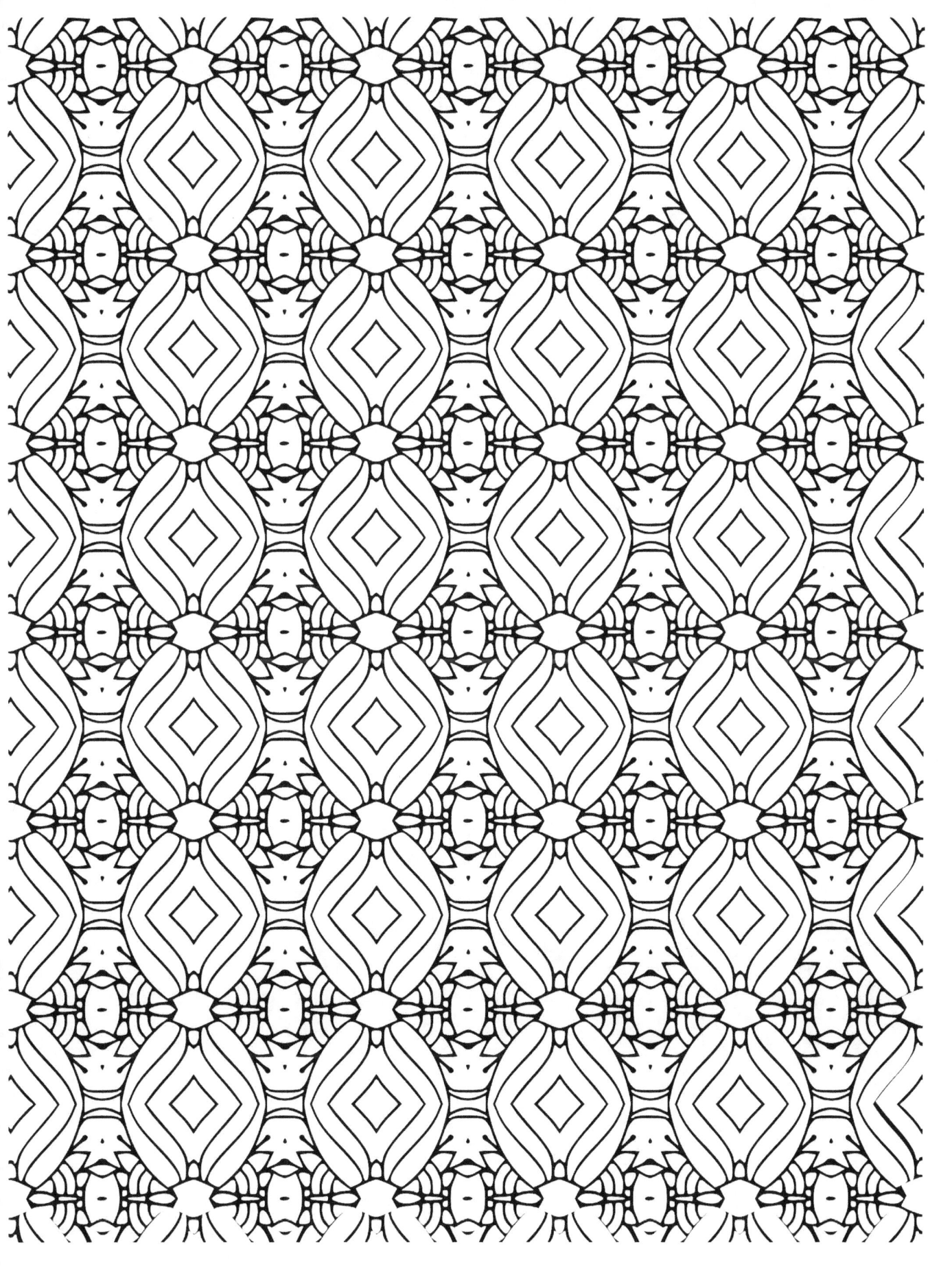

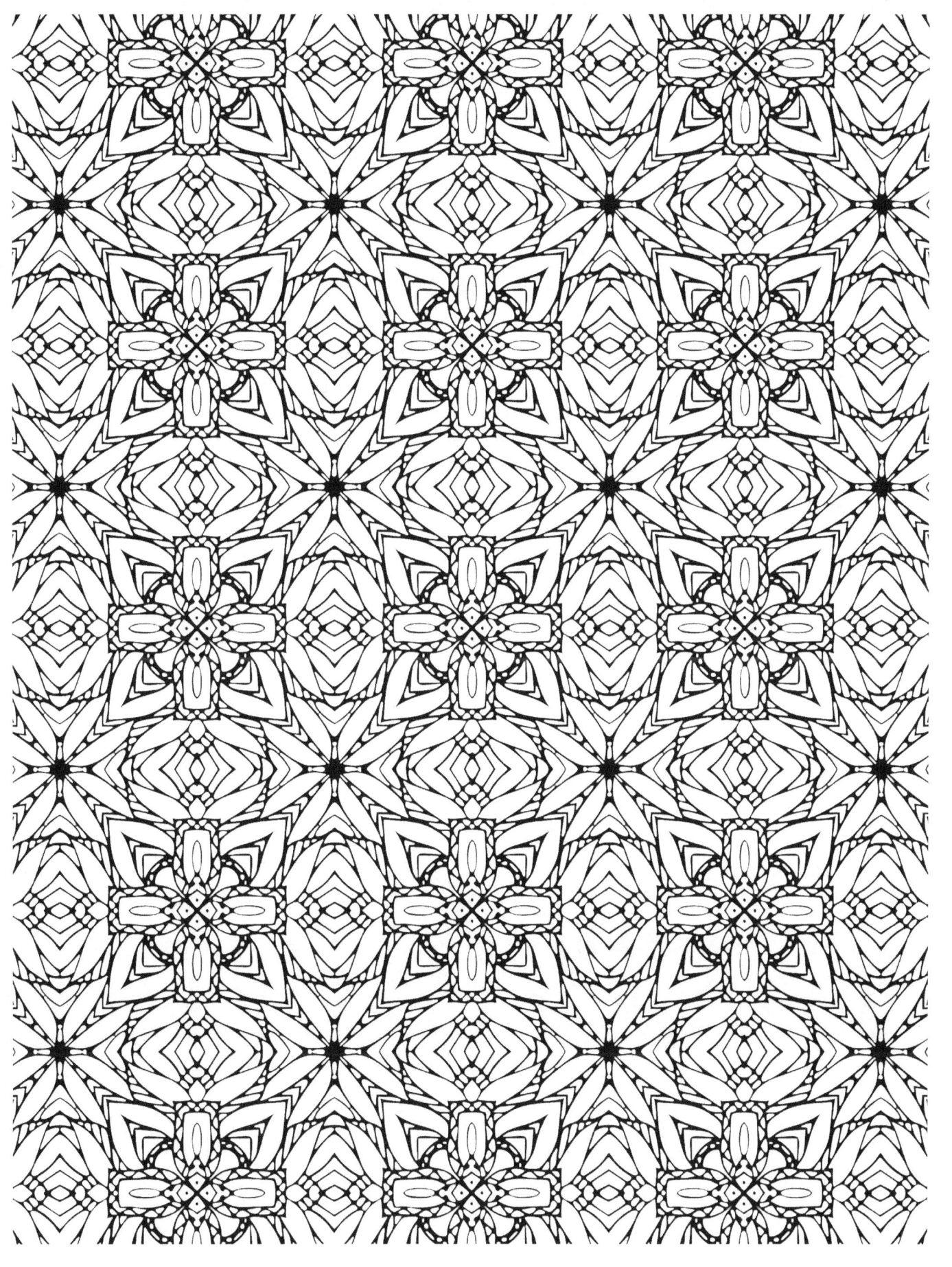

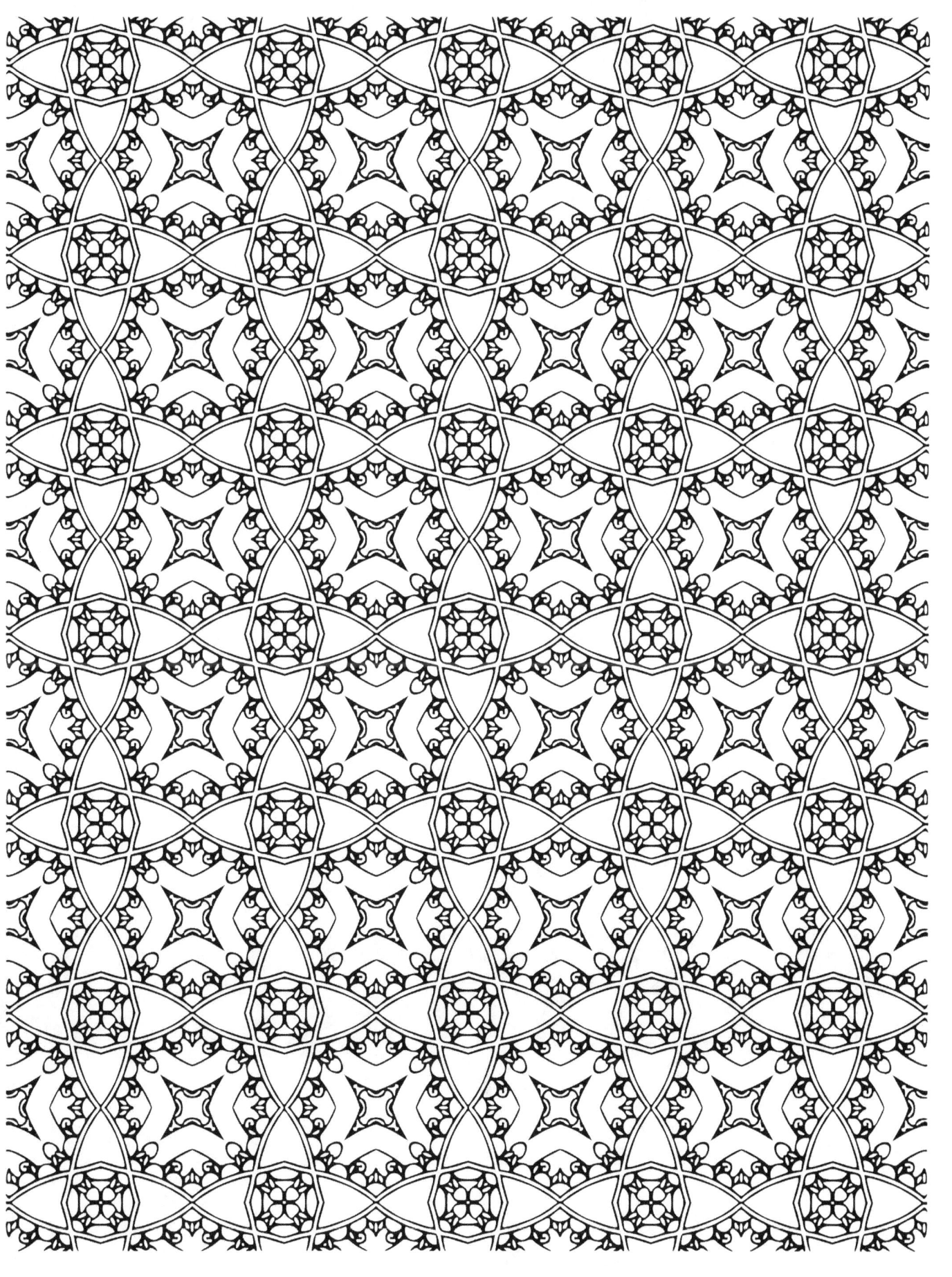

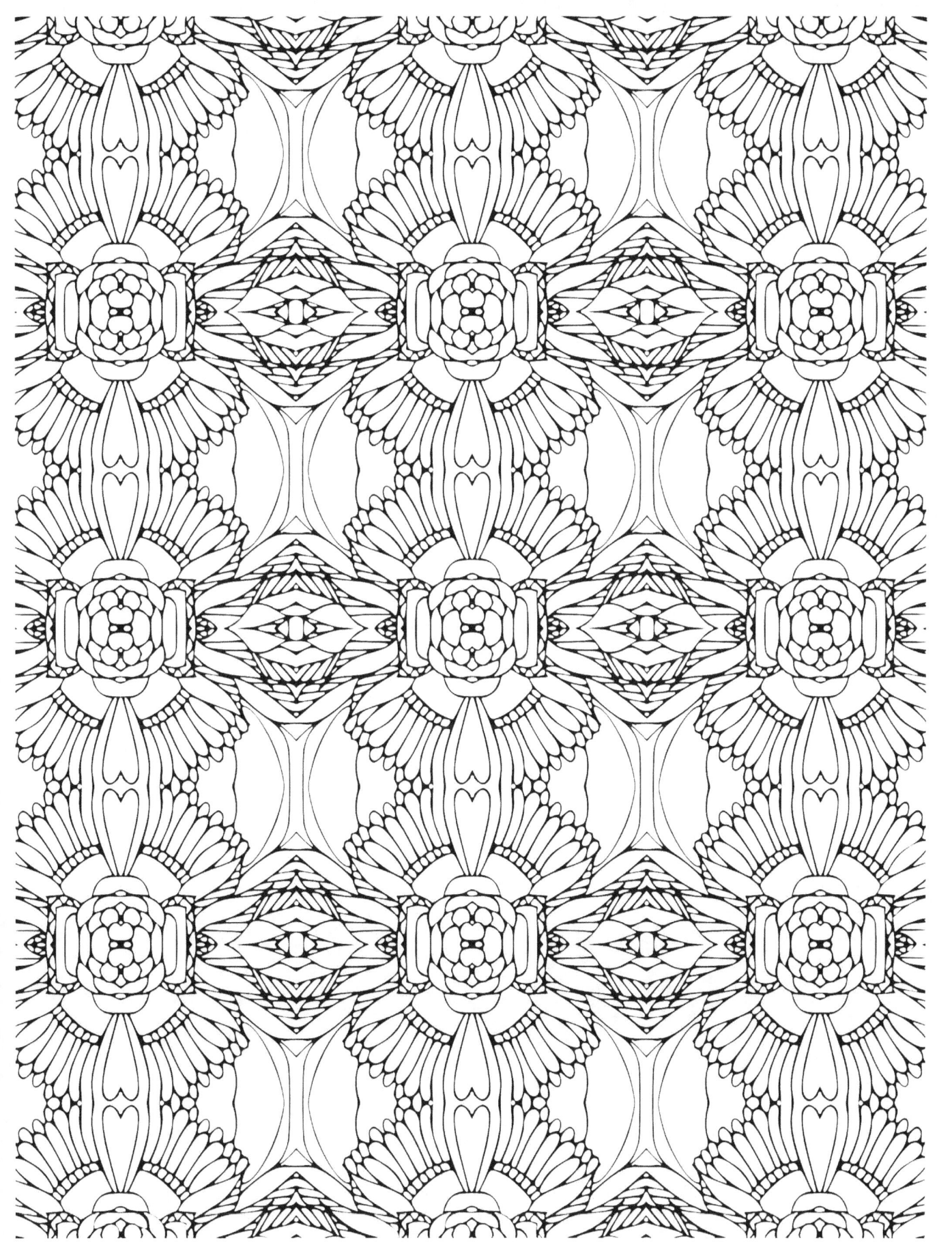

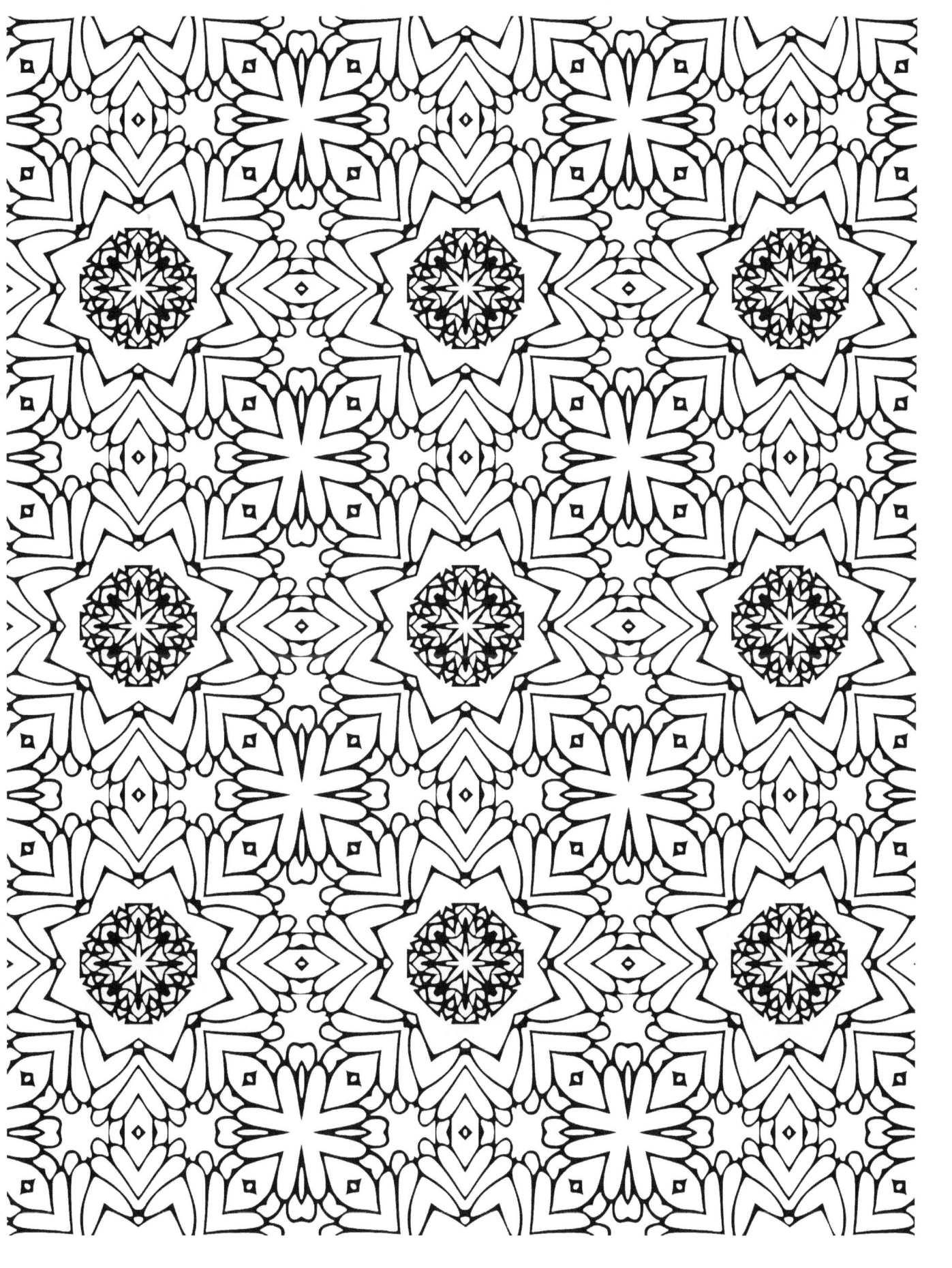

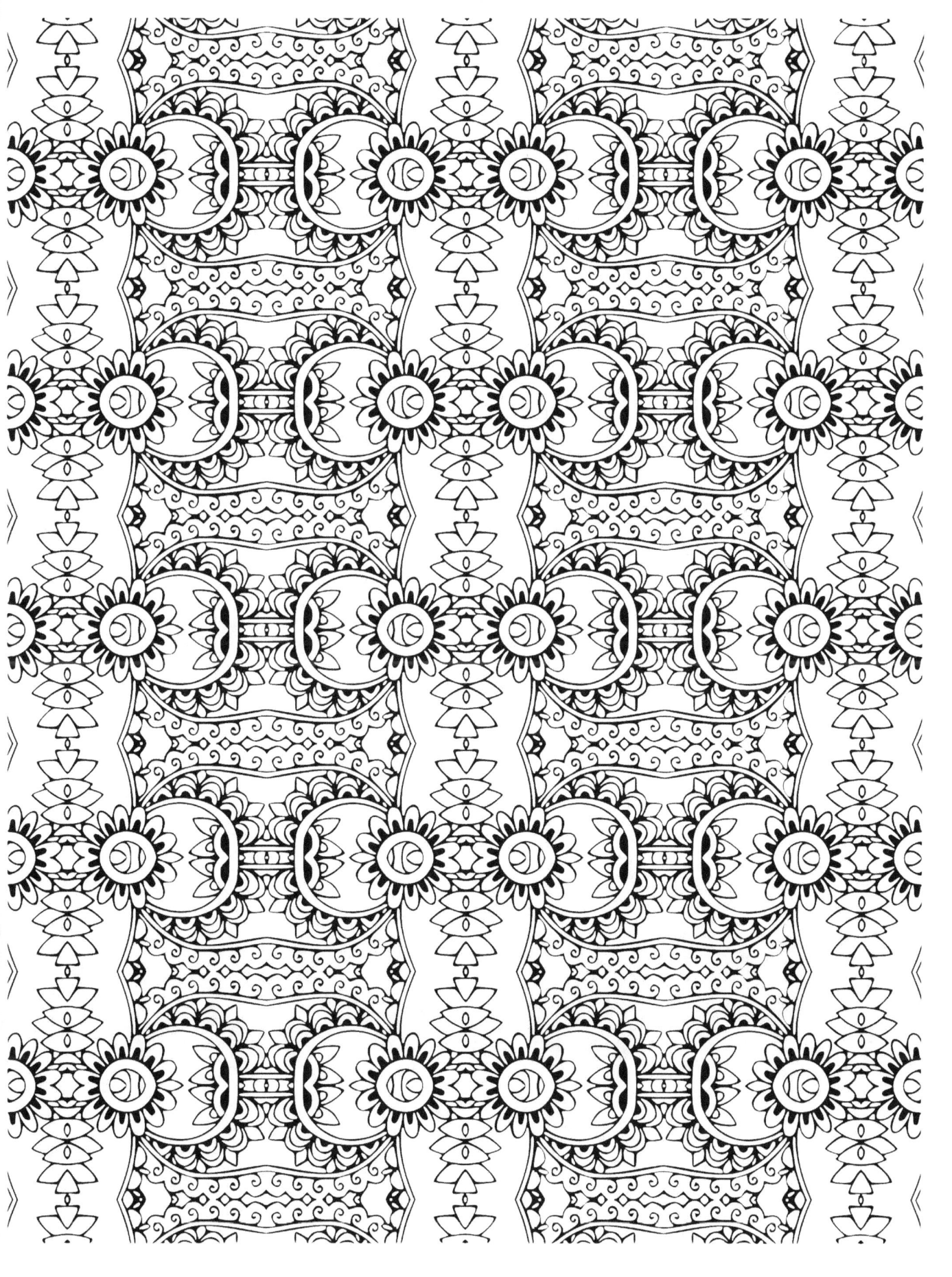

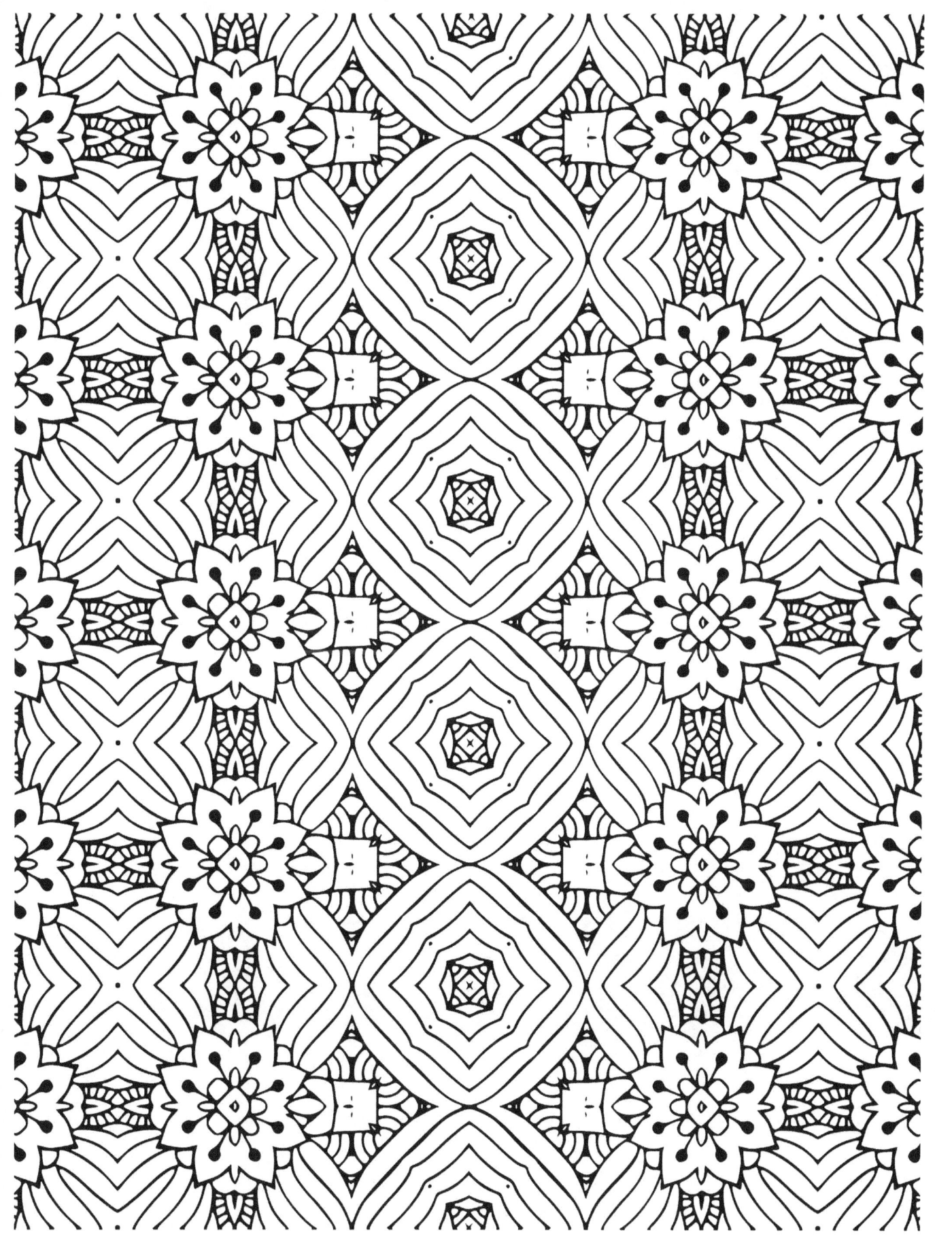

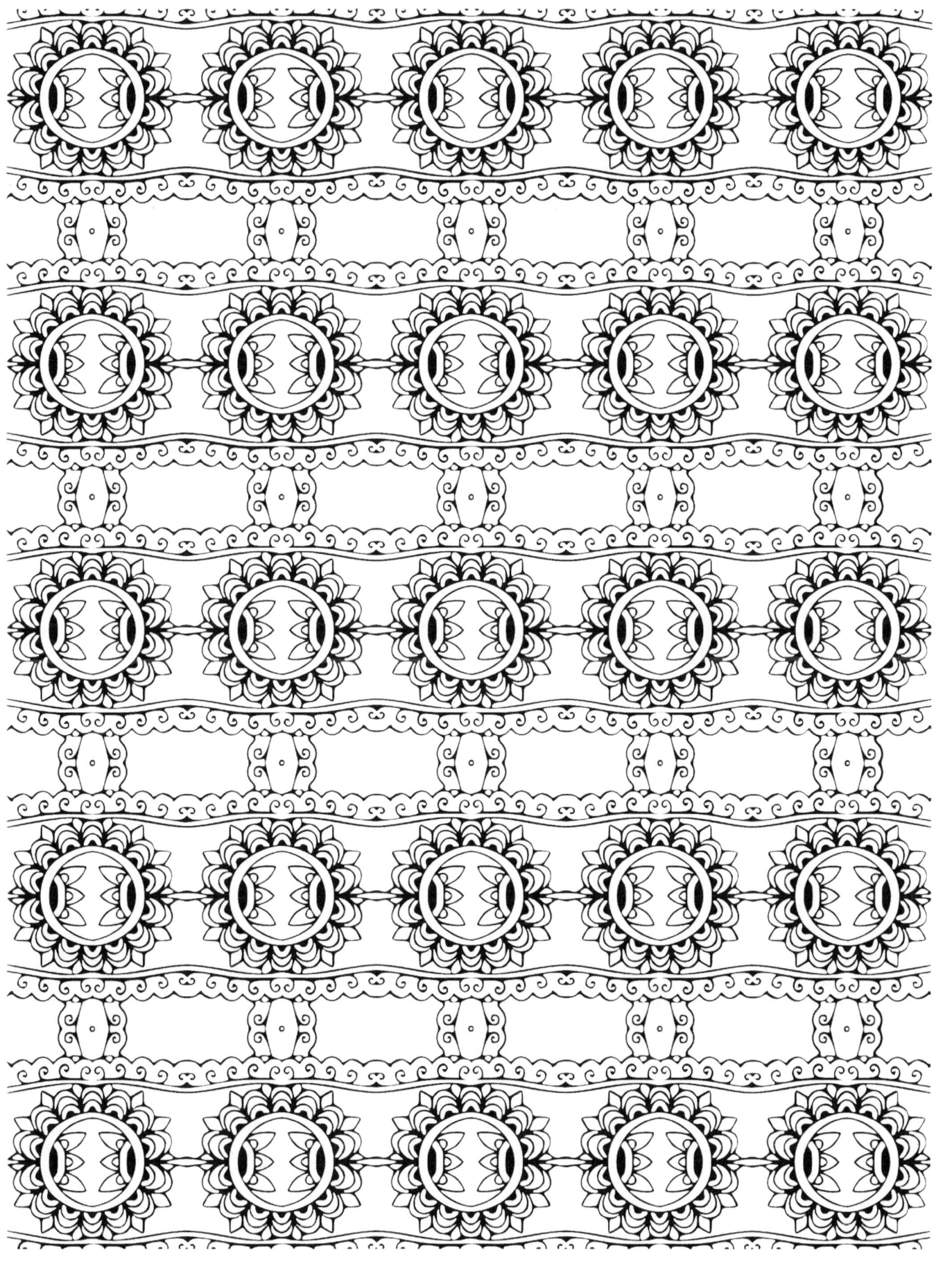

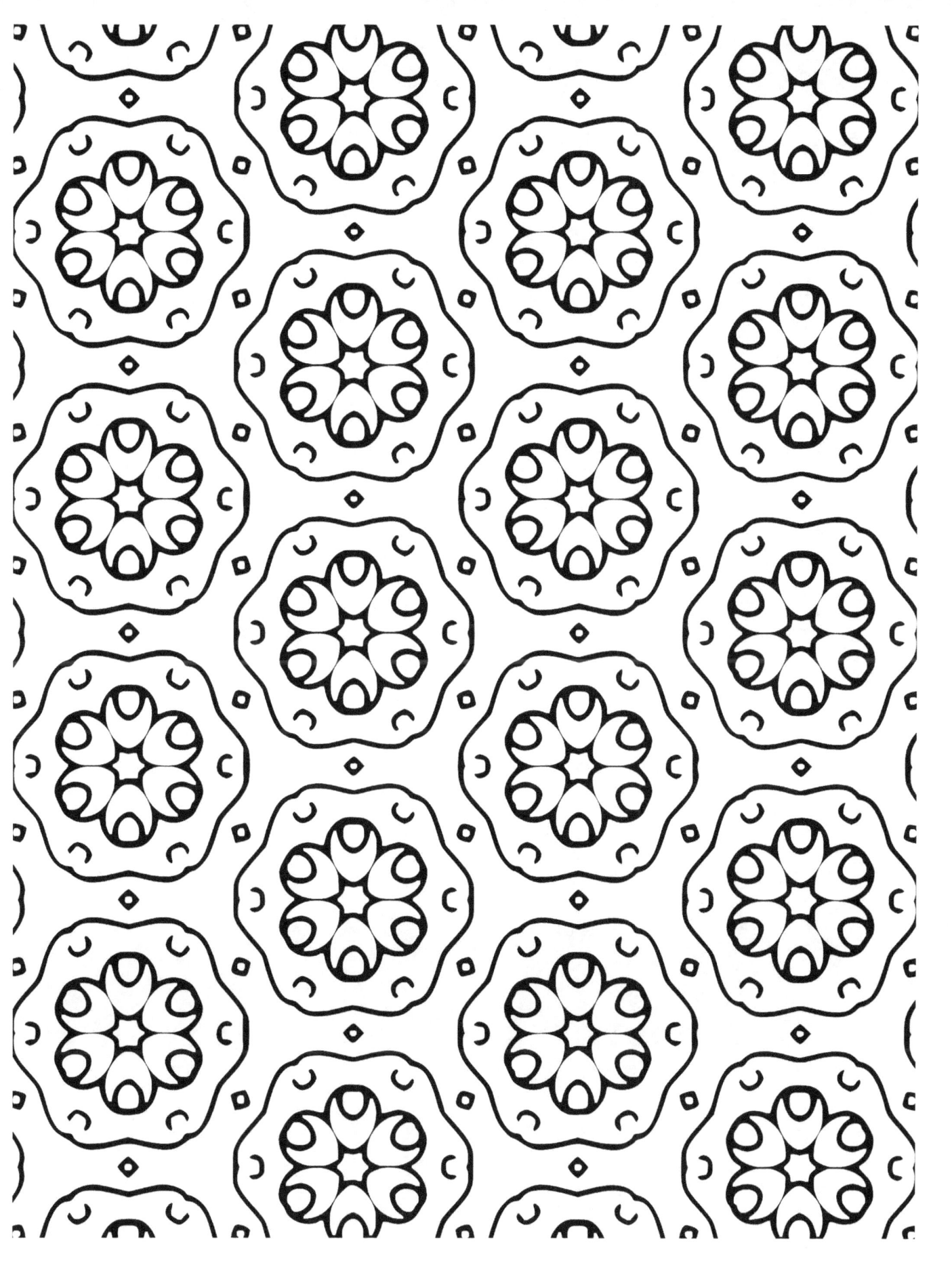

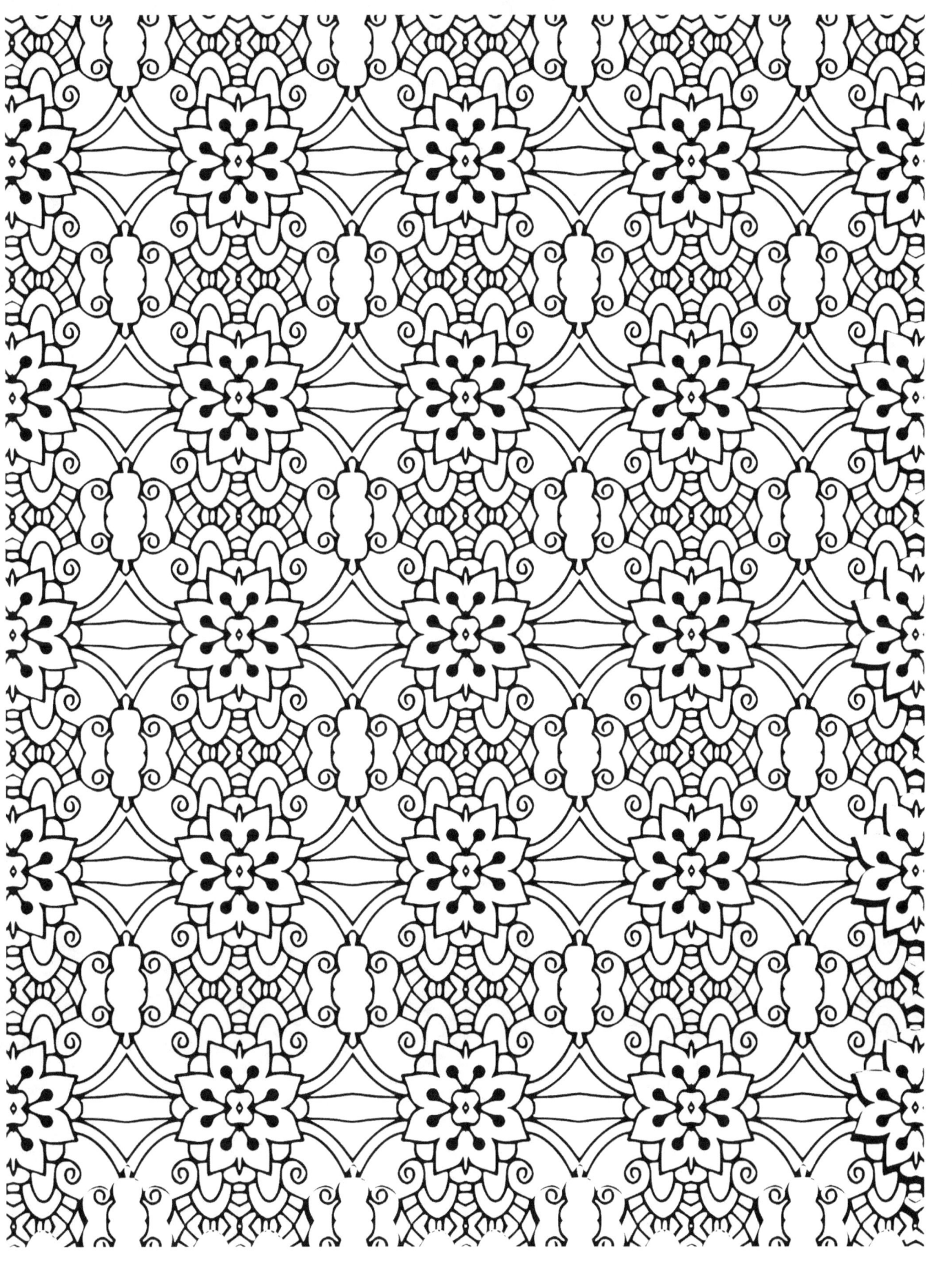

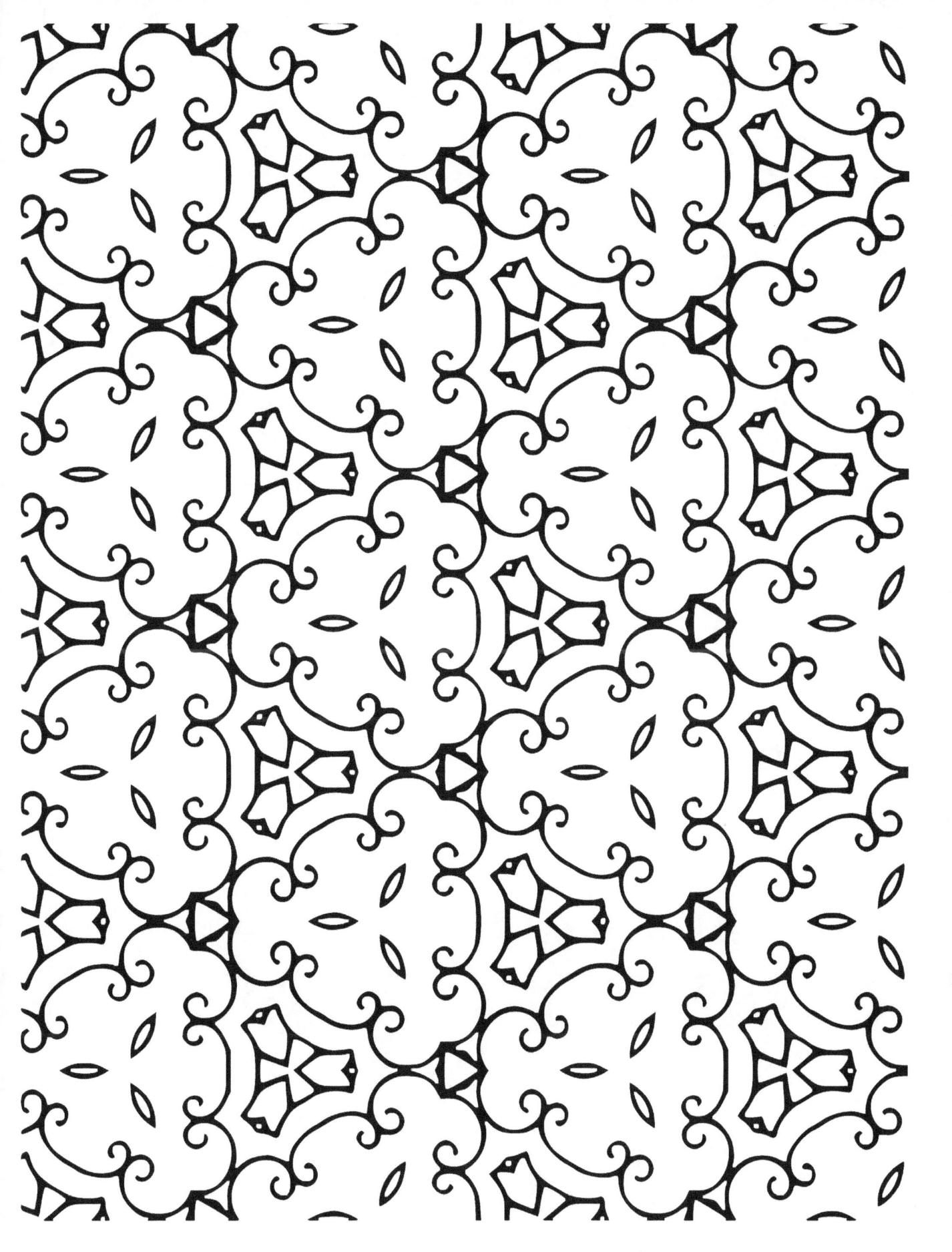

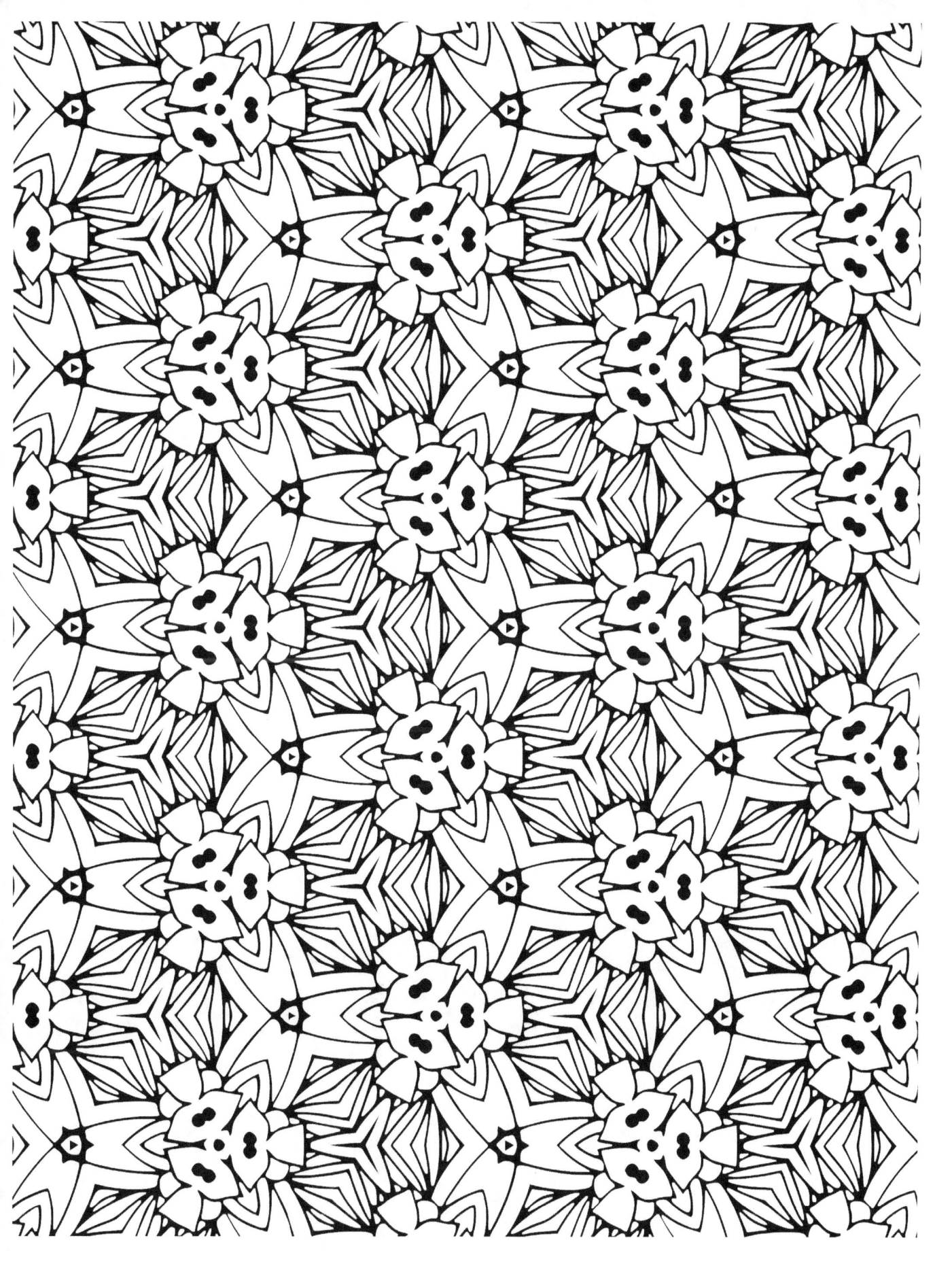

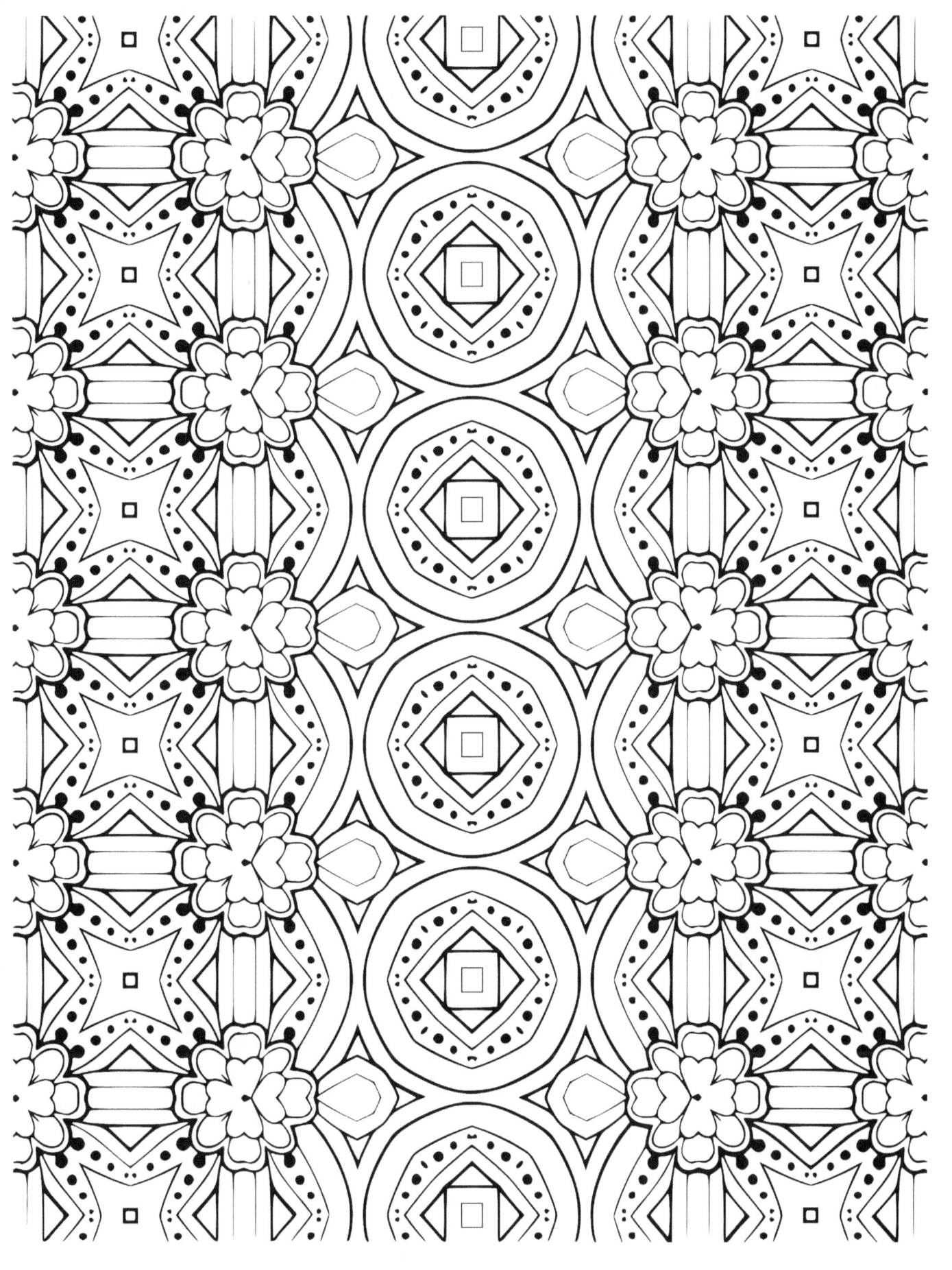

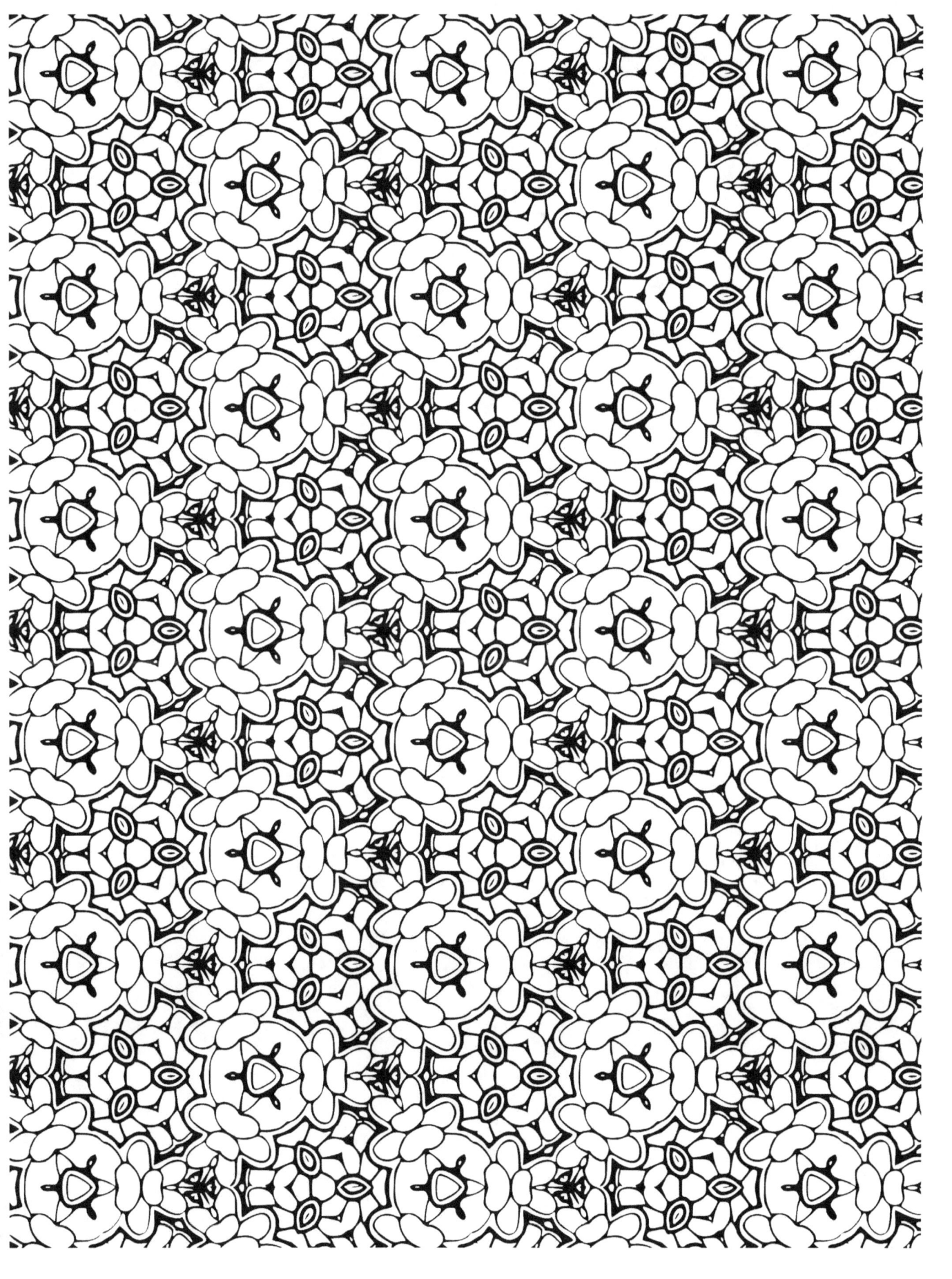

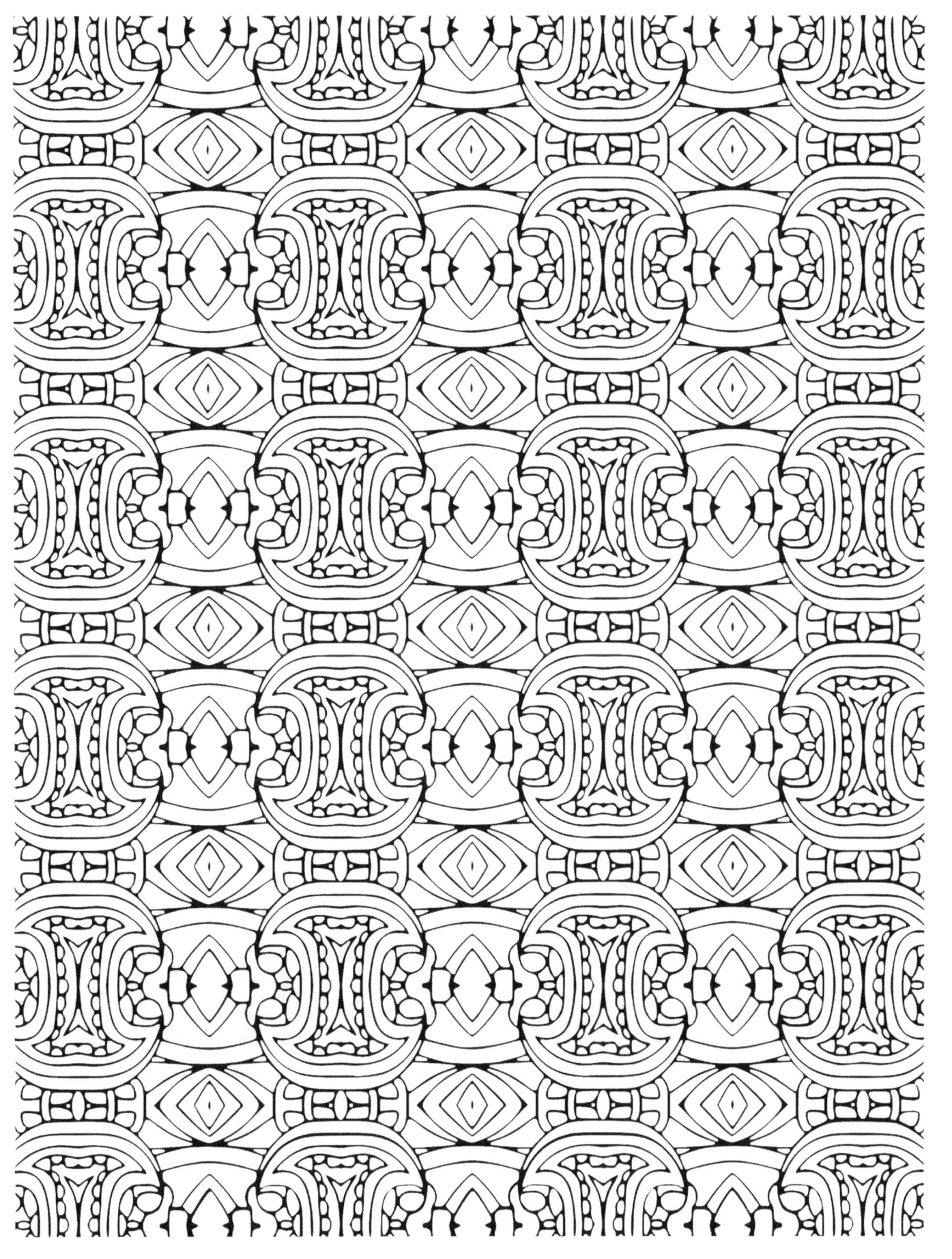

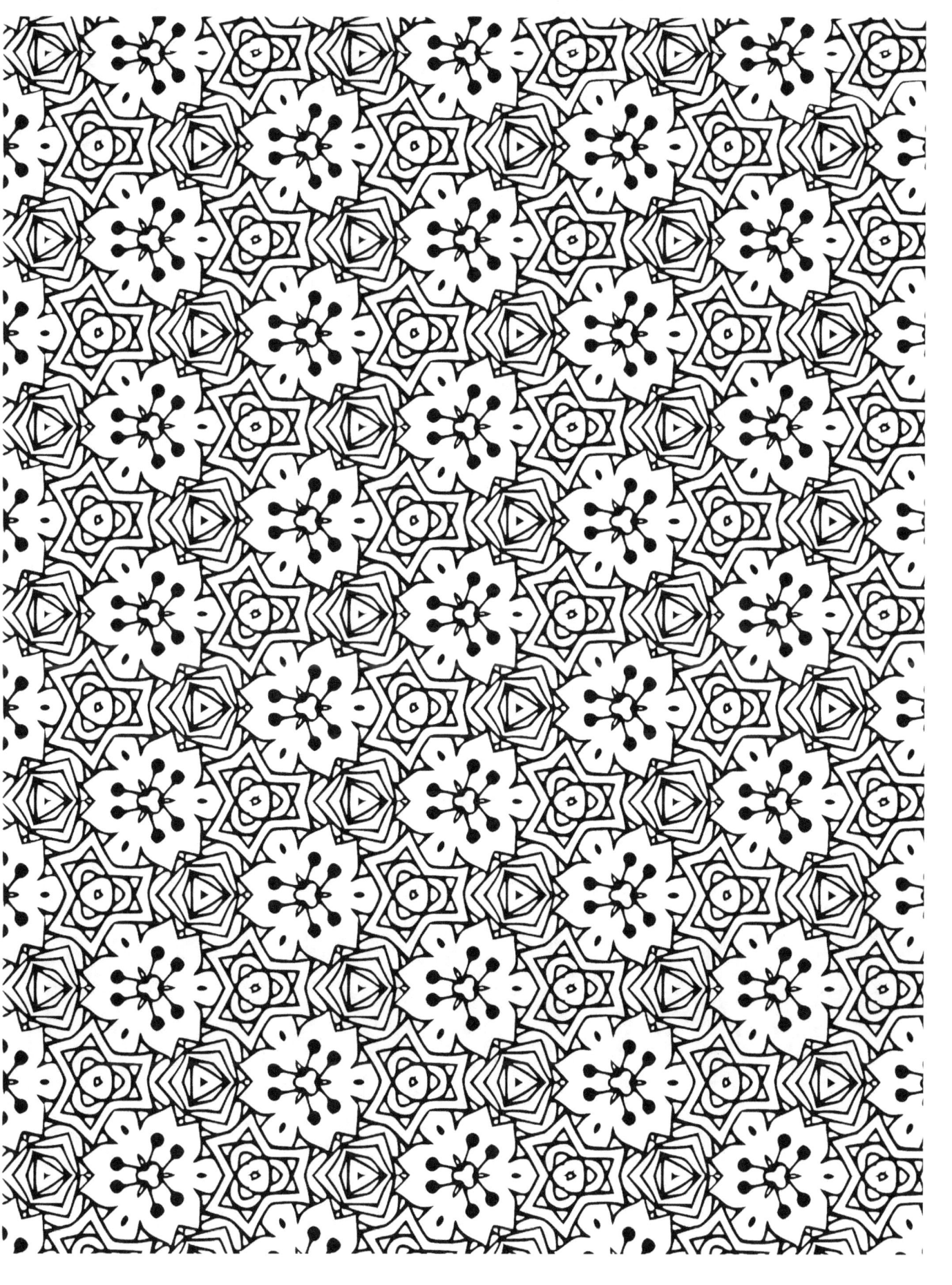

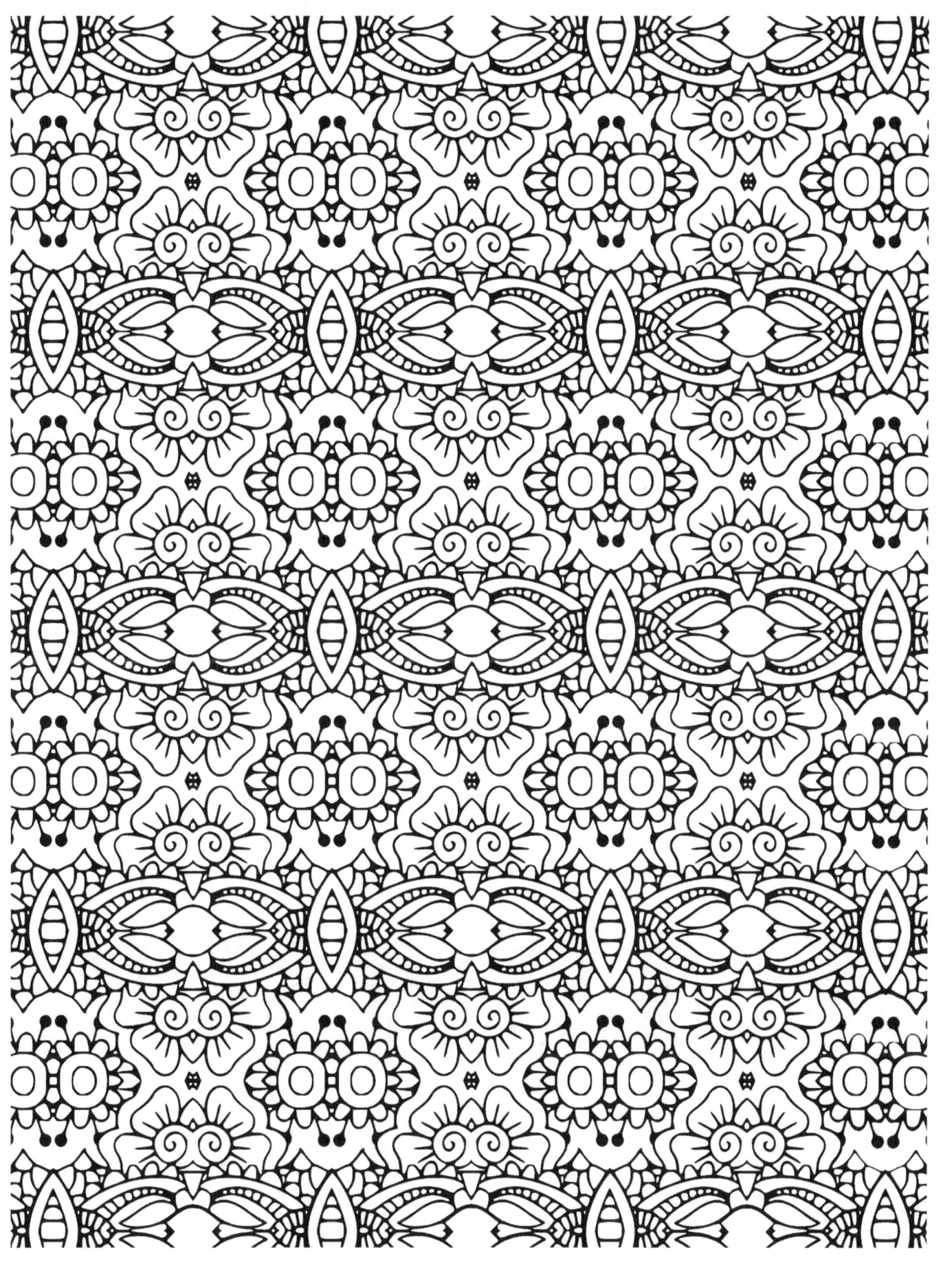

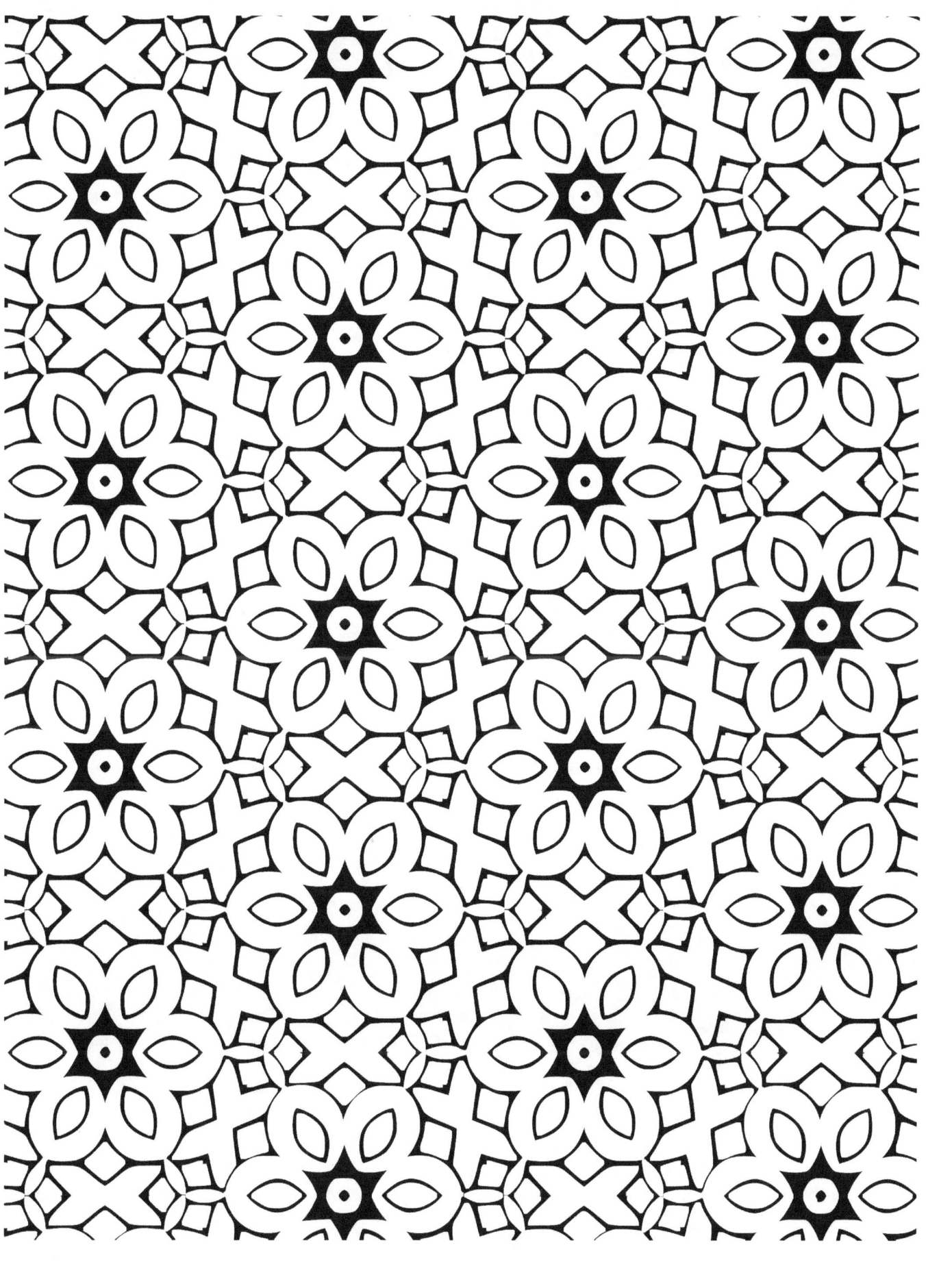

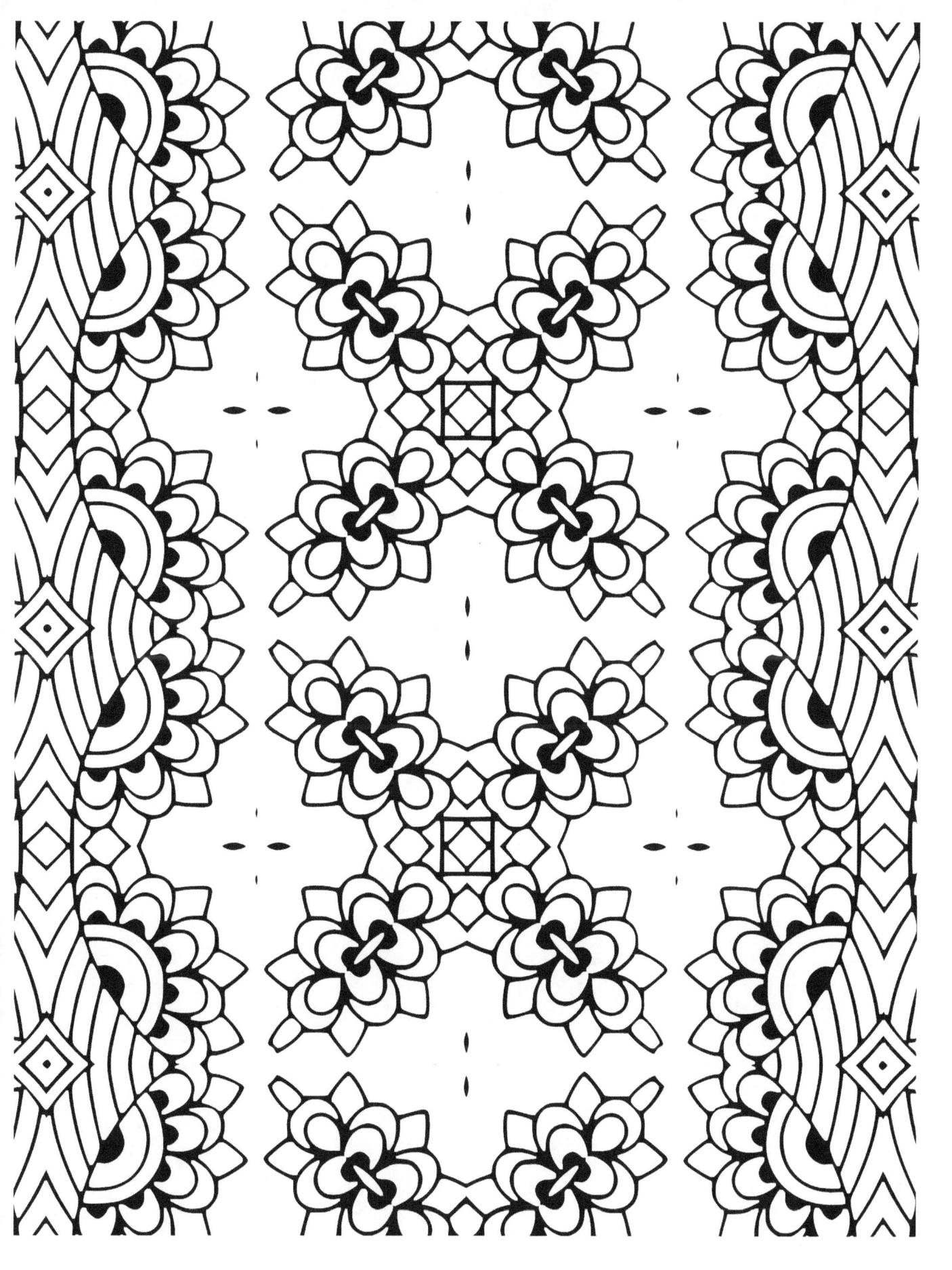

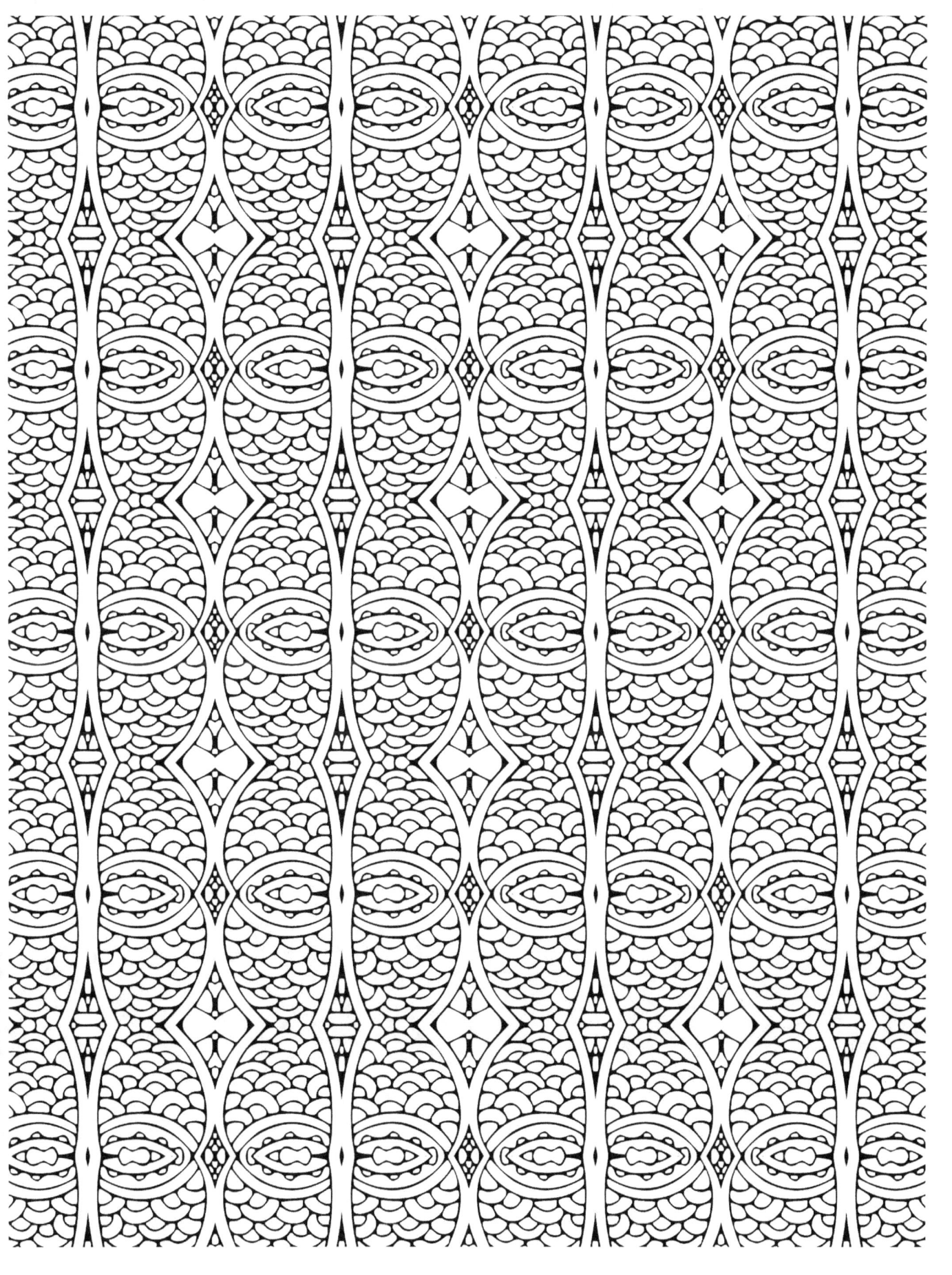

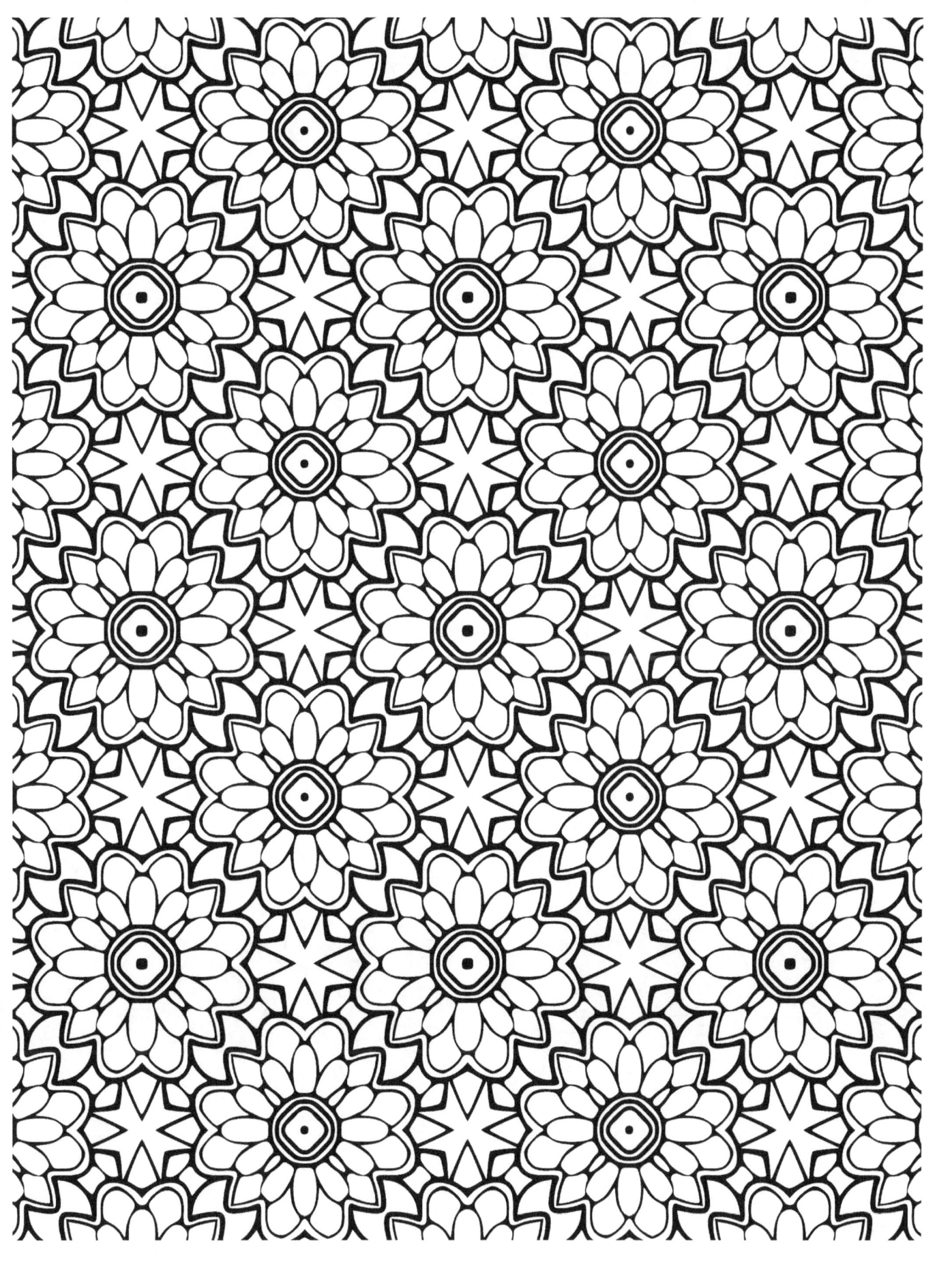

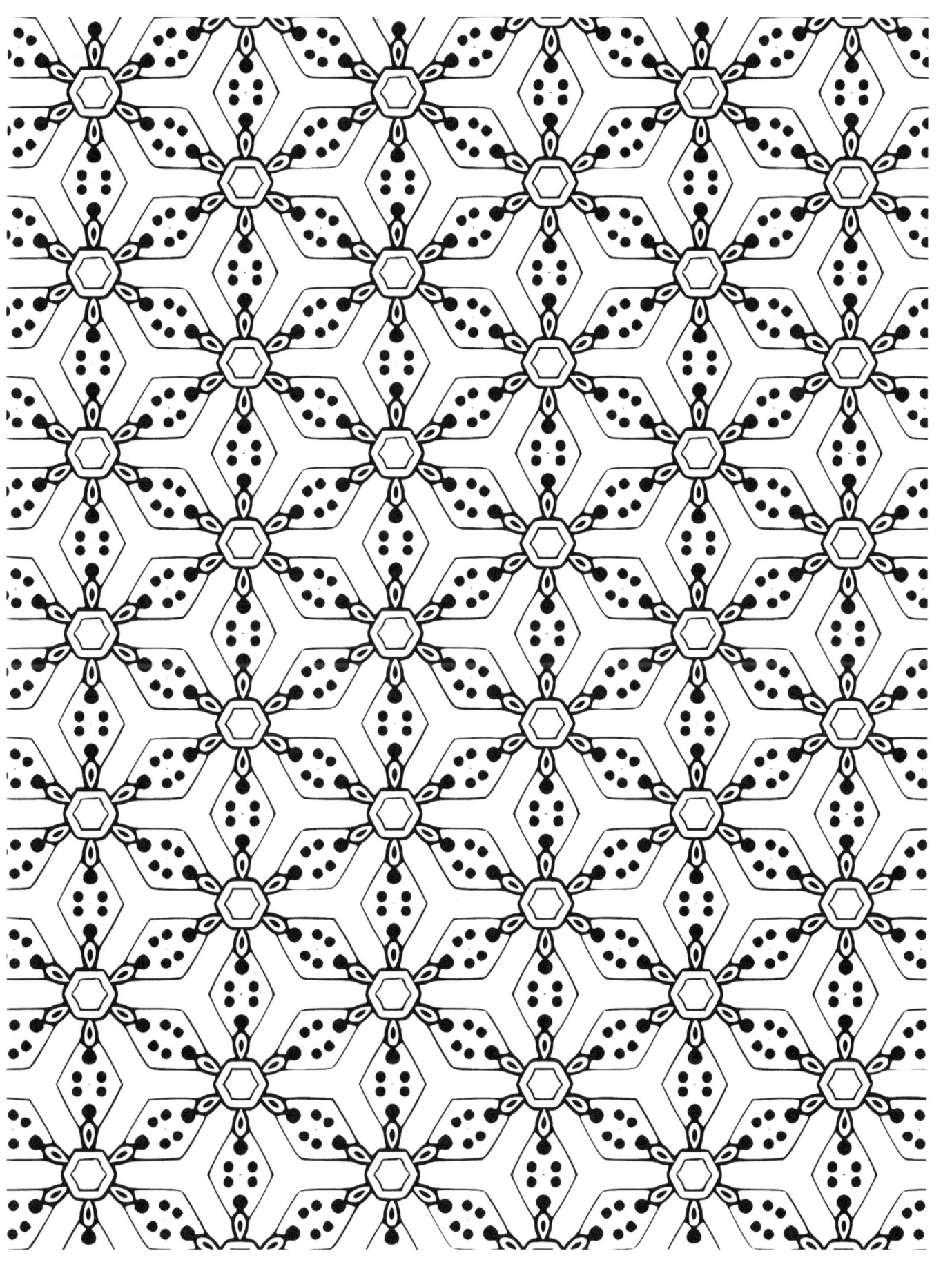

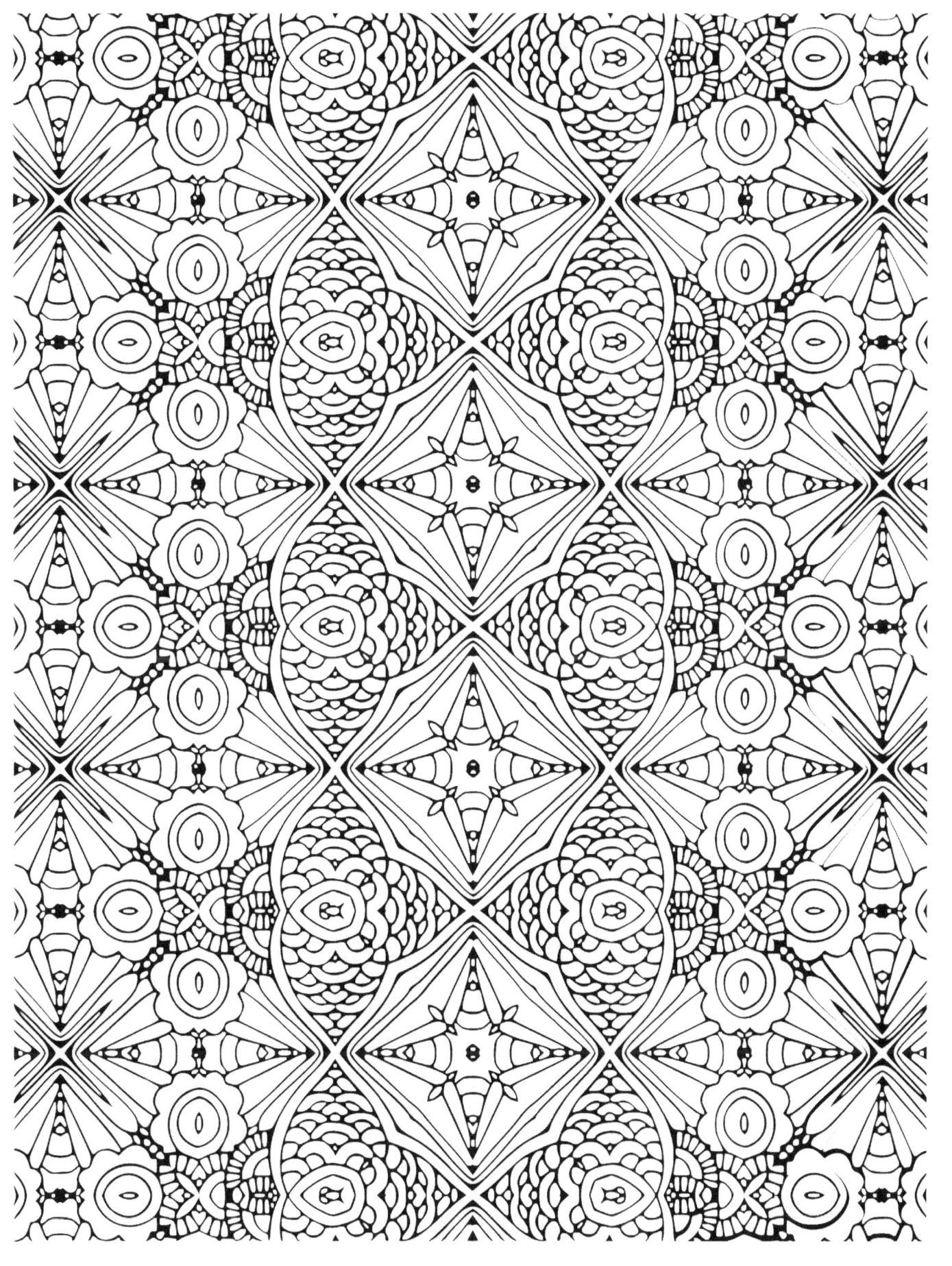

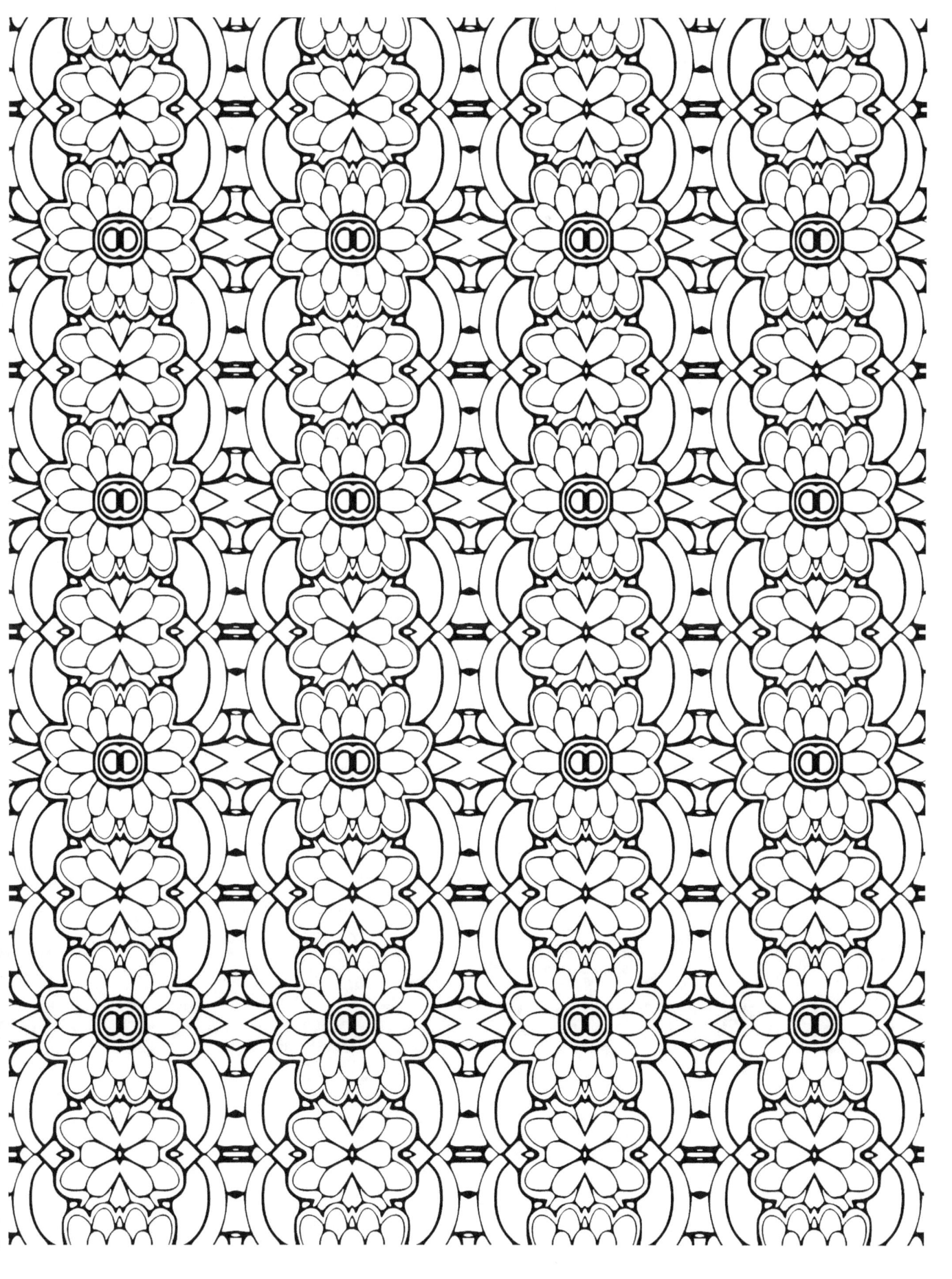

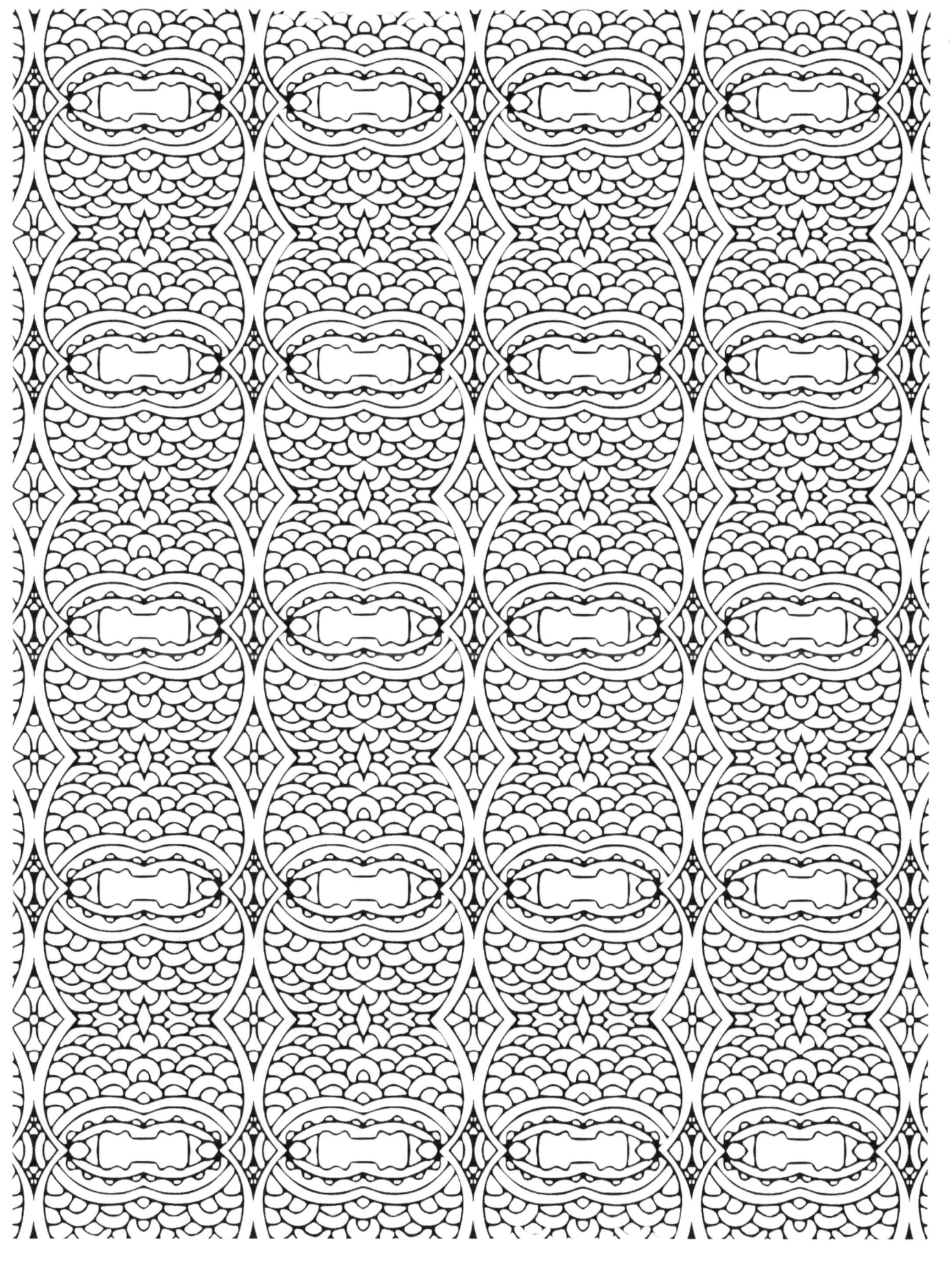

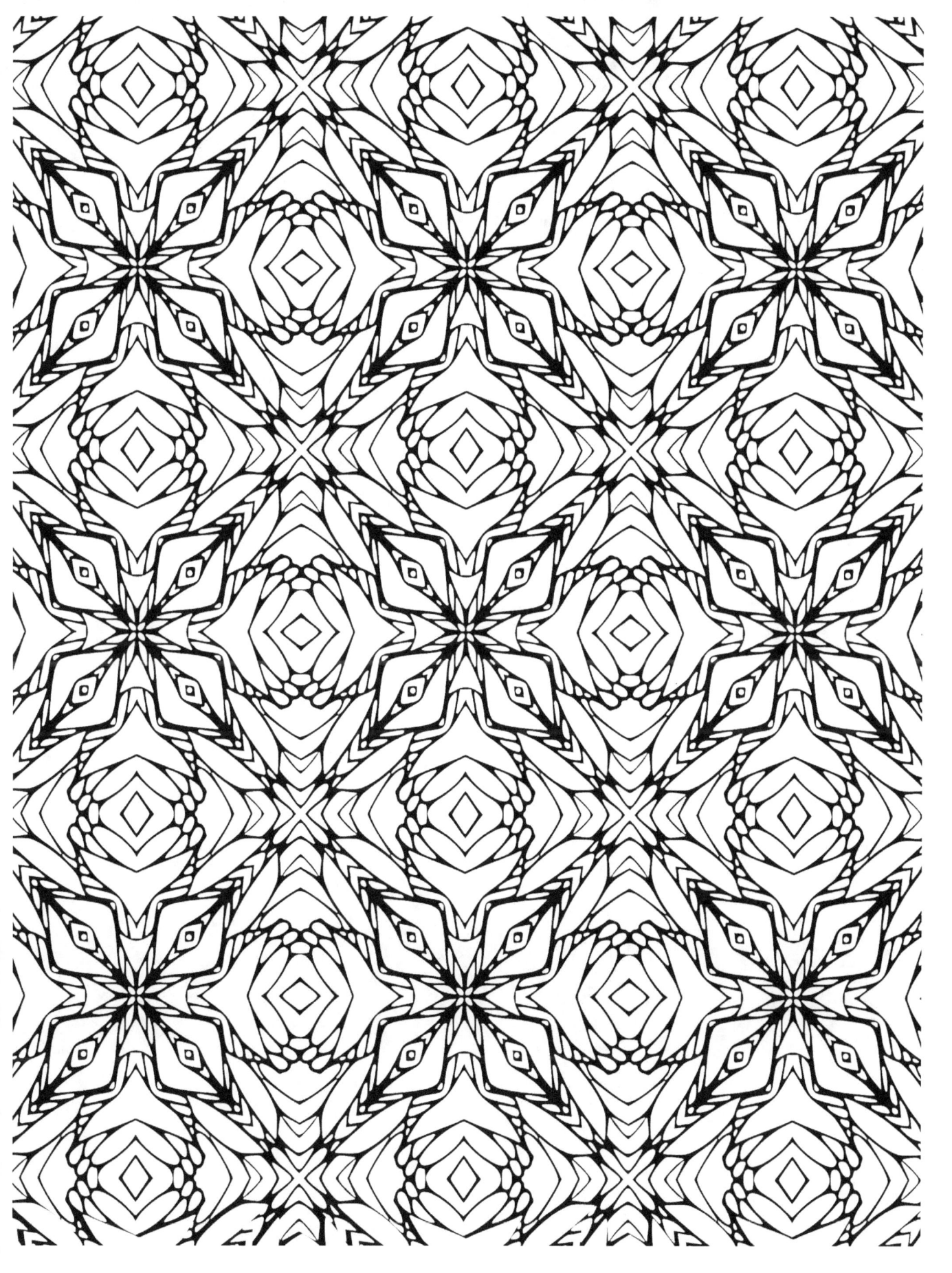

www.ingramcontent.com/pod-product-compliance
Lightning Source LLC
Chambersburg PA
CBHW080720190526

45169CB00006B/2455